GUJARAT FILES

ANATOMY OF A COVER UP

RANA AYYUB

First published in 2016 by:
Rana Ayyub
rana.ayyub@gmail.com

Dedicated to Mukul Sinha and Shahid Azmi
who gave me a purpose to fight.

For Abba and Ammi

CONTENTS

Foreword   vii

Preface   ix

Chapter 1   1
Chapter 2   11
Chapter 3   32
Chapter 4   52
Chapter 5   71
Chapter 6   80
Chapter 7   110
Chapter 8   126
Chapter 9   149
Chapter 10   166
Chapter 11   201

FOREWORD

हिरण्मयेन पात्रेण सत्यसापिहितं मुखं ।
तत्त्वं पूषन्नपावृणु सत्यधर्माय दृष्टये ॥

(The face of truth is covered by the golden vessel;
Oh Pushan, uncover it for the vision of truthful dharma)
—Ishavasyopanishad

'Truth is stranger than fiction, but it is because Fiction is obliged to stick to possibilities; Truth isn't', said Mark Twain epigrammatically. But, the nature of truth, has baffled philosophers all over the world for ages. Like the Holy Grail, it is envisioned differently by different persons in different times and tracts. People who pursue the truth single-mindedly must of necessity tread the lonely path beset with travails and tribulations bereft of expectations of help from anyone except their own conscience to guide them.

This version of the truth of the disturbing events in Gujarat during 2002 and the saga of fake encounters makes fascinating reading. According to the author, this book gives the reader an insight provided by the lens of a spy camera and spy microphone both of which were freely used in a long drawn sting operation. As to whether the material presented in this book represents facts, or mere perspective vision of the events, is for the reader to judge.

The narrative interspersed with quoted conversations makes interesting reading. It is for the State apparatus enforcing the Rule of Law and the Constitutional machinery as its sentinel to objectively assess the trustworthiness of the facts narrated here and take necessary action to restore the faith of the citizens of this country in the Rule of Law.

With the painful experience gathered from the Commission of Inquiry that went into the riots and the violent incidents in Mumbai during December 1992–January 1993, and the sense of apathy towards the victims of such riots that was clearly discernible, one feels that it is time that the State machinery and Constitutional functionaries displayed greater seriousness in investigating the causes of such riots and took appropriate steps against their recurrence.

While one may not be in a position to validate all that is narrated in this book, one cannot but admire the courage and passion displayed by the author in her attempts to unmask what she believes to be the truth. Kudos to her and her brave assay in investigative journalism, the need for which seems to increase with increasing dishonesty, chicanery and political machinations.

Mumbai,
11 April 2016   B.N. SRIKRISHNA

PREFACE

The struggle of man against power is the struggle
of memory against forgetting.

—*Milan Kundera*

A haunting memory that remains an integral part of my life
has to do with reporting for a news channel some time in
2007 about the rape of a three-year-old girl who was in a
municipal hospital. Her parents who sold pirated books at
a traffic signal seemed to be under the influence of drugs,
and hence were unaware of the pain and misery of one
of their five girls. Her face and body were badly bruised,
the savagery on display all over the tiny, innocent frame. I
reached home at two in the night after sending in the tape
of the story to the Delhi studio. I remember inundating the
investigating officer in the middle of the night with messages
to check if the perpetrator had been caught. The next day
I reached the hospital to see if the girl was recovering.
She had developed multiple infections, flies swarmed on

her wounds while needles perforated her tiny wrists. Her parents were still not in sight. When I reached my office I urged my boss to play it big so that the criminal was caught and brought to justice. He just smiled and continued gazing at his laptop. It was raining profusely and my boss asked me to focus instead on the Milan Subway and the rains and get some good shots of the floods.

'I cannot do this,' I screamed at my mother when I called her on my way to the Milan Subway which is a favourite with camerapersons in Mumbai during its famed monsoons. My heart was pounding, I had not been able to eat all day. The third day after the incident my family doctor had to give me a sedative. I called up my editor suggesting that I needed to take a week off. I had been working on an investigation of the Students Islamic Movement of India (SIMI) just prior to the story about the little girl, and had had major arguments with him over ethics and morality in journalism. He gave me a patient ear and then said something which stayed with me.

A good journalist should learn the art of detaching herself from a story and be pragmatic. Till this day I regret being unable to master this art. Particularly because very often, it is used as an excuse to kill a story at the behest of corporate and political powers.

CHAPTER 1

The summer of 2010 was to redefine journalism for me. I considered myself a hardworking, mediocre reporter with a set of ideals passed on by an old-school journalist father. But at this time, I found myself at a crossroads I wish and pray no journalist is ever brought to.

I had resumed work at *Tehelka* after a long medical leave some time in 2010. Doctors across the city could not diagnose my condition. I had returned from an assignment in the Naxal heartland of Gadchiroli recently. The story preceded what I consider one of the most shattering incidents in my life. The assasination of a very dear friend, Shahid Azmi. One of the finest minds in criminal law, Azmi had come to assume a significant role in my life. On the evening of his death, I was to meet him to discuss the case of tribals and intellectuals who had been labelled Naxals by the establishment and were languishing behind bars on false charges.

But fate had other plans. I stayed back at home at the

insistence of my niece. It was her seventh birthday. There were dozens of missed calls on my phone, messages that asked me if I knew 'what the latest was on Shahid', which I saw only later. The rest was conveyed to me by incessant phone calls from friends and the breaking story on news channels. Shahid had been shot dead at his office by unknown assailants for taking up cases of 'anti-nationals'. Shahid's arguments had recently led to the acquittal of innocents in the 7/11 Mumbai train blasts. After his death, Mumbai courts acquitted the two co-accused in the 26/11 Mumbai attacks. The mastermind behind Shahid's assassination remains a mystery to this day, at least in the public eye.

There are various ways to cope with one's loss. You either mourn and move on. Or you run away from it, and try to find solace in your work. I chose the latter. The third day after his death, I was on my way to Nagpur, for what would turn out to be one of the most important stories in my journalistic career. It concerned the arrest of students mostly from backward classes on charges of being Naxalites. The evidence against them was laughable. They possessed literature on Bhagat Singh and Chandrashekhar Azad. It felt like remittance to me, because my friend Shahid had died representing cases similar to this. In my mind, it was my tribute to his memory. But fate had other plans. I returned home soon after to an inexplicable ailment, which was later diagnosed as depression.

The diagnosis was made after my paranoid parents got me to undergo every kind of test. From bronchoscopy to

MRIs. Another doctor suggested that my parents start me on medication for tuberculosis. But as luck would have it, I chanced upon one of Mumbai's most acclaimed physicians in a South Bombay hospital. Dr Chitnis saw my reports and asked me some questions. Then he took a deep breath and asked, 'What's bothering you?' It was as if his words woke me from a stupor. 'Nothing doctor, I am just too drained and feel weak, can't figure out what's happening?'

With a vague smile on his face, he said, 'Get rid of this self-pity, stop glorifying your misery with these blood tests, you are absolutely fine. Get back to work, that's your panacea. It's all in your head.'

'Is it hypochondria?' I asked. I had come across this term very recently while trying to self-diagnose my condition. 'No, you are just being plain lazy and running away from your responsibilities,' said Dr Chitnis nonchalantly

The next couple of days I tried to make sense of Dr Chitnis's recommendation. It was on one of those lazy days that my mother decided to play the catalyst. Amma, as I call her, has been one of my most loyal friends . She never really saw modern schooling, Abba was her teacher. She said she wanted to live her dreams through me. I would rebel, she would fight, connive for me and eventually everyone at home would come around. That day as she served me coffee she asked, 'So are you quitting your job?'

I shrugged, only interested in the cup of coffee that she had got along for me. Then true to her character, she sat down next to me on the bed and started reading the *Inquilab*(a prominent Urdu daily). Ten minutes into reading the newspaper she had just begun to ask me something, when I stopped her midway, ' Amma, if it's some sermonizing that your newspaper carries today, please don't bother, am better off without it.'

'Arre nahi, did you read about this Sohrabuddin?' she asked. For some reason that name piqued my interest. Of course I knew about Sohrabuddin, I thought to myself. He was the reason behind my first interaction with one of the most controversial figures of our times, Narendra Modi.

In 2007, three of Gujarat's top cops were in the news after they were arrested by one of their closest colleagues Rajnish Rai for having killed Sohrabuddin, a small-time crook, in a fake encounter.

D.G.Vanzara and Rajkumar Pandian were behind bars. They were the most trusted officers of the Modi dispensation, and had until then lived in glory, with newspapers flaunting their pictures at press conferences every day. They were the officers who had successfully tracked and managed to kill jihadists on their way to assassinate Narendra Modi, the Hindu Hridaya Samrat earlier in 2004. Their arrest naturally attracted national attention.

Having secured a job as a political journalist in 2007 with a television news channel, the first task at hand for me was to cover the 2007 Gujarat elections. Narendra Modi, the Chief Minister of Gujarat, was on his way to what most analysts predicted as another sweep. The 2002 riots in Gujarat that had polarized the society had made him a hero among the majority Hindu population. A victory sweep in 2007 did not look very difficult for him.

Accompanied by a cameraperson I found myself at his first election rally. I don't clearly recollect, but I believe it was organized by the Gujarat Chamber of Commerce. Narendra Modi was on stage with his Man Friday Amit Shah by his side, apart from other ministers.

There were other political rallies too which I had covered and this seemed no different at first. But as my producers back in Delhi had told me, Modi had a knack for making provocative speeches. And that day he didn't disappoint. 'Sohrabuddin, they ask me what do I do with a terrorist like Sohrabuddin.' The crowds cheered. The ladies in the front row clapped; that row was always reserved for them as it was believed that Modi was popular with women in Gujarat. Columnist Aakar Patel even wrote in a column that for Gujarati women, Modi was a sex symbol.

The response from the crowd was on expected lines: 'Kill him, kill him'. To me it seemed like a Roman amphitheatre. The speech continued with odious references to 'Miya Musharraf' and 'Dilli ki Sulatanat'. When he had finished speaking, Modi stepped off the dais and was garlanded by the Gujarat Chamber of Commerce members. The crowd gathered around him. I squeezed in, past his security cordon, screaming anxiously at my cameraperson who struggled to get in behind me.

'Modiji, Modiji, ek sawaal'. As luck would have it, the man who was being escorted by his fans and entourage turned to look at me in acknowledgement, expecting possibly a political question. 'Modiji, three officers have been arrested in Gujarat and have been charged with the fake encounter of Sohrabuddin. Would you still justify what you said in your speech?' Expecting a response, I turned my mic towards him. But this turned out to be the cameraperson's moment. Narendra Modi stared at me for a good 10 seconds and then walked away. His minister gave me a look of disdain. This was my first encounter with the man now holding the most coveted position in the country, that of the Prime Minister.

The Sohrabuddin story clearly had to be told. And the opportunity had presented itself to me via my mother reading her copy of *Inquilab*. On an instinct I went to the local cyber shop.

All links related to Sohrabuddin spoke about a CBI investigation into the case and the arrest of one of Gujarat's top IPS officers, Abhay Chudasama. I was familiar with Chudasama; just about an year ago he had threatened me on the phone after I had published a confession by one of his star witnesses in the Gujarat blasts case. Chudasama was the officer in charge of the Gujarat blasts investigation, which was eventually linked to the group called the Indian Mujahideen. One of the most articulate and media-savvy officers in the state, Chudasama, it was rumoured was close to the Gujarat Minister of State for Home, Amit Shah. But Chudasama was different from others who had shot to fame. He was, as would be revealed later, a man who was more comfortable dealing with crooks and hawala accounts. And Sohrabuddin turned out to be one of his own henchmen.

With printouts and my notes ready, I wrote a note to

Shoma Chaudhury and Tarun Tejpal, my editors back in Delhi, about the case and the need for it to be reported. At the back of my mind, I knew this could be my way out of the self-imposed isolation and depression that had gripped me. Both my editors were more than encouraging and I set off for Ahmedabad again. This was a visit that turned out to be a life changer for me.

Within a month of my visit I made two important exposés by digging out call records and internal notes with the help of officers who shall remain unnamed. I approached them cautiously, knowing fully well that they were my only hope. But trust does not come easy in a state like Gujarat where officers who had decided to go by the call of duty had to suffer the wrath of the government. Most of them were also meeting me for the first time. To make matters more complicated, I was a *Tehelka* journalist, which roughly translated into the supposition that at any given point in time I would be armed with a sting camera.

What I had encountered in Gujarat though was not a Gujarat-centric issue. Prosecution of honest police officers was routine in Uttar Pradesh and Manipur as well, two states I had extensively reported from. I also realized that the same prosecution factor would turn out to be my saviour. As it turned out, the officer who would go on to reveal some of the most incriminating notes to me turned out to be a batchmate of an official I had reported about. That broke the ice. With able help from human rights activists and officers who provided me with evidence, I made one of the most sensational exposés of the year. These were the call records of the then Minister of State for Home Affairs, Amit Shah, and top officers during the course of encounters. Accompanying the call records was a damning internal Official Secrets Act note. The minister's activity was being monitored by the state CID and the note alleged that the encounter was a sinister plot to kill innocents and label them terrorists.

The exposé created ripples in the political fraternity. Phone calls from the CBI poured in asking *Tehelka* to hand them those records which were later placed before the Supreme Court. I continued to stay at Hotel Ambassador in Ahmedabad, which by now had become my second home. Located in the predominantly Muslim locality of Khanpur, this was a rather unassuming place for me to stay at. I would discover later that the state BJP office was only blocks away. I was suddenly in the public eye. BJP leaders spoke about a certain young chap called Ayyub who had made the disclosure. For some reason the idea of a female investigative journalist had not crossed their minds. I was not complaining, it only allowed me to go about my work discreetly. But this did not last long. A few days into the exposé, my phone received a text from an unknown number which read, 'We know where you are.'

Life had indeed changed; from that day on I changed my accommodation every third day, from the IIM campus in Ahmedabad to guesthouses, hostels, and gymkhanas. I had begun to operate like a fugitive. By this time, landlines had replaced mobile phone communication for me. Finally having provided all the evidence I could dig up to the CBI and writing my follow-up reports, I landed in Mumbai and decided to get back to some semblance of routine.

But destiny had other plans for me. Within weeks of the exposé, the CBI arrested Amit Shah, the first serving Home Minister in the history of independent India to be arrested. It became an overnight sensation. Most of the national media parked itself outside the CBI headquarters in Gandhinagar. As expected I had to return to Gujarat and report on the developments that followed the sensational arrest.

Shah's arrest gave a new lease of life to those police officers who had been discriminated against during his rein. Officers sent feelers to me at this time saying that they wanted to talk. Many who had earlier avoided journalists now gathered the strength to speak. While most conversations were off the record, it was clear that the encounters were only the tip of the iceberg. There was something more sinister that had been buried in the files of various cases in Gujarat. None of us were anywhere close to the truth. There was an indication that over the last decade there had been subversion of the judicial process. Those who were supposed to safeguard the lives of people had been bought over. From the riots to encounters to political assassinations, many an inconvenient truth was waiting to come out. But how could one prove any of it?

The basic rule of journalism was evidence and I had none. There were only conversations and anecdotes, off-the-record confessions. How was I to prove it all? It was then that I made the decision that would change my life, professionally and personally. Rana Ayyub had to give way to Maithili Tyagi, a Kayastha girl from Kanpur, a student of the American Film Institute Conservatory who had returned to make a film on the development model of Gujarat and Narendra Modi's rising popularity among NRIs across the world.

CHAPTER 2

An elaborate mail to my seniors and an encouraging response from them to probe deeper was enough to set me thinking. Close to three months in Gujarat and the circumstances under which I had met those willing to help me with information was indication enough for me that the road ahead was tough. To cull the truth from individuals who were in a position of power and had chosen to seal the truth within themselves was not going to be easy. My colleague at work Ashish Khetan had made chilling revelations in his exposé in which he had stung the likes of Babu Bajrangi and other local BJP and VHP leaders as they mouthed a cold-blooded narrative of the riots in 2002. But I was not up against the rioters who would speak of their bravado at the slightest ego boost. I was dealing with seasoned, senior IPS officers many of whom had had successful stints with RAW and I&B.

These were thick-skinned diplomats; to get them talking would require the skills of an able and astute investigator armed with power and authority. I did not qualify on any of these counts. Besides the planning, the execution too had been left entirely to me. I was aware that I could not take a junior from my office for that would only mean added risk. It was made clear to me that my editors would monitor my work but everything else had to be my responsibility. Every time I sent in a transcript I would get encouraging responses from both Shoma and Tarun with phrases like 'excellent, keep at it' or 'stunning revelation'. While it encouraged me to probe further, the truth was that I was a lone soldier on the field. I had to look after myself and ensure that the investigation yielded honest, fact-based results.

There were people who knew the truth and had chosen to live with it, going about life as if this incident, the cold political bloodbath that had taken place in 2002 was not a part of their career. As a journalist with an investigative organization like *Tehelka*, I knew every door that could have offered some help was closed to me. The only way out before me was what every journalist in the pursuit of truth uses as a last resort. Go undercover. I was all of 26, a girl, a Muslim girl at that. I have never been conscious of my identity, but when it came to a state polarized on religious lines, these considerations were to be considered judiciously. My family was to be told about it, who would I be? Would I be able to pull it off without help?

The fact that I had attended a well-known mass communications course came handy at this time. Among my classmates were aspiring actors who had carved a niche for themselves in the film industry. Actor Richa Chaddha who was my classmate and now one of the finest heroines recently mentioned in an interview that she chose my career graph and experiences as a journalist to prepare for a film that had her play the role of a reporter. That 'long time no see' call was made to another actor friend I considered myself closest to. With my friend's help, I fixed an appointment with her make-up man. The next day I was sipping chai at a suburban Mumbai studio learning the technicalities of getting myself the right wig. The make-up artist, who turned out to be a veteran, helped me with some of the ones he had stocked. The wigs made me look different, but something felt cosmetic and out of place. The wig makeover had been a non-starter.

I thought a better idea would be to focus on changing my identity altogether. As luck would have it, I found an email on a group ID that I was a part of with my ex-classmates from a colleague who had joined the prestigious American Film Institute Conservatory in Los Angeles. It felt like an Eureka moment. This was to be my identity. A filmmaker from America in Gujarat to make some sort of film. The idea was ambitious, but the possibility of it working was within the realm of possibility.

I spent the next few days studying the work of the conservatory, its alumni, the films it had made and doing research on the kind of films that had been made about Gujarat, and the subject they had most focused on. Finally, I decided to keep the subject of the film open-ended depending on the kind of reception I received from the characters I would meet in the story which had no script.

I had to have a name. One which was warm, conservative and yet strong in what it had to convey.

I must confess that being a film buff did help me immensely. I love watching Hindi films and one of the films that I remembered seeing at that point was Rajkumar Santoshi's *Lajja*. I had managed to watch it on a flight from Delhi to Mumbai. The strong female characters in the film were its USP, backed by powerpacked performances by its lead, including Madhuri Dixit and Manisha Koirala. In the film, Koirala played a character called 'Maithili' who explored the lives of Indian women and caste- and gender-based suppression. Maithili was also the name of Sita, wife of Lord Ram. The name had a resonance that had stayed with me. When I found myself looking for a second name, which was common and without the snob value of some surnames, indicating neither Brahmin nor Dalit status, 'Maithili Tyagi' was born. My visiting card read Maithili Tyagi, Independent Filmmaker, American Film Institute Conservatory.

But before I left for Gujarat again, I needed an able assistant who came along soon enough and whose presence would have a deep impact on my life. Mike (name changed) was a Science student in France who happened to be in India on a student exchange programme. Mike wanted to work in India with Indian journalists. I mailed him without giving him the precise details of the investigation that I would be conducting, yet trying to be as honest as possible.

I told him that I needed a non-Indian colleague who could pretend to be working with me on a film. This, I informed him, would be part of a larger, more sensitive investigation. Mike would not be privy to the intricate details, I warned him. He would just be a 'firang, gora' face to authenticate my identity.

Armed with my visiting cards, a pair of ash-grey lenses, a hair straightener, colourful bandanas and some recording instruments, I landed in Ahmedabad. Mike was to arrive a couple of days later. I immediately procured a sim card in the name of Maithili Tyagi. I was surprised at the ease with which I managed one with the help of documents arranged by my alleged 'guardian family' in Ahmedabad. The investigation was to take a long time. Neither I nor my organization could afford the luxury of accommodating me in a plush hotel. Also I was playing the role of a struggling filmmaker who had limited financial support. Accommodation for someone like that could be arranged only by a local. This time help came from an artist friend who was well-connected in the literary and cultural circles in Ahmedabad. He was kind enough not to ask too many questions. That I was a journalist who had sent the HM of Gujarat behind bars on account of her investigation was reason enough for him to use his influence to help me get accommodation at an educational institute, the Nehru Foundation.

I was introduced as a filmmaker to the warden of the hostel at the Foundation who barely glanced at me and had an animated chat with the friend who was helping me. I had successfully secured myself a 250-sq-ft-room with an adjoining washroom for 250 rupees a day. As it happens, the fellow occupants at the hostel played important roles in my investigation. They were students from different parts of Europe—Germany, Greenland and London.

Manik bhai (name changed), the dean or the manager of the hostel was my first acquaintance. 'Madam is here to make a film on Gujarat' is how my friend introduced me to him. 'Oh nice' remarked Manik bhai, 'Please say good things about my city and our CM. It's a beautiful city, this Ahmedabad,' he said offering to show me around the city in the same breath. My room had space enough for a single bed, a writing table and a book stand. But the location of the hostel made up for the lack of space. Situated in one of the most plush and central areas of Gujarat, this place became my home away from home over the next six months.

Mike arrived the following morning, a bright tall French boy, all of 19, with messy hair. I met him at my friend's place where I briefed him about his role before he accompanied me to the hostel.

Manik bhai was kind enough to give Mike a room adjacent to mine for the next one month. That Mike impressed him with his 'Kemchho' obviously played a role in this. Mike was a learner, and loved exploring and learning about cultures, but his particular favourite was food. Our first dinner that evening was at the popular thali joint in Ahmedabad called Pakwaan. As Mike and I now fondly remember, he must have finished off at least two dozen pooris and six bowls of halwa that night much to my puzzled amusement.

As we walked up the stairs of the hostel after dinner, he asked, 'So can I call you Rana, when we are by ourselves?'

'No, I will be Maithili for you till you leave this country.'

Mike kept his promise. The goodbye card that he left for me a day before leaving for Paris had a note scribbled in Hindi, 'Pyaari Maithili, apna khayal rakhna—Mike'.

We spent the first few days at the Nehru Foundation getting accustomed to our new lives. Mike would sit in his room with his French-Hindi translation book while asking me questions and simultaneously reading a book by Mark Tully. For his age, Mark was very well-read, opinionated and had an incisive, analytical mind. He was quick to grasp details. We had a canteen at the Foundation which served lunch for 25 rupees. It overlooked a carved staircase and the institute terrace beyond which lay a picturesque forest. Every afternoon Mike and I would carry our laptops to the terrace eating our lunch and working simultaneously. He would ask me, 'So Maithili, what's the plan, who are we going to meet?' And I would repeat myself, 'I will tell you, when the time is right.'

In the evening Mike and I would take our cameras out and go to the old city to shoot. Both of us shared an interest in photography and both had similar SLR cameras. The exercise had nothing to do with our love for photography however. It was an exercise in strengthening the authenticity of our roles for ourselves, and anyone who might have been watching us. If we had to approach top-ranking officials, there would most certainly be a background check especially at the place where we were staying. We needed to have a social circle in Ahmedabad which could vouch for our assumed identities.

Amdavad ni Gufa, the historic art museum set up by the

famous artist M.F.Hussain turned out to be of great help for us. The museum surrounded by a huge park and a café had youngsters, mostly artists and photographers lounging around. Some played the guitar, some promoted their work. Others included aspiring filmmakers, photographers and theatre actors. During our evenings at this place, I would thoroughly enjoy my life as Maithili and so would Mike.

Mike loved the Lal Darwaza, a prominent part of Old Gujarat. Every Thursday there would be an open market there. Then there were the kite makers and the potters. He would come back in the evening with some spectacular shots and then pop his favourite question, 'Where are we eating tonight?' He was a foodie and Gujarat was just the right place for him.

In the meanwhile help arrived in the form of an email from an activist friend. I needed to establish some sort of contact with the officers, and the first in my list was G.L.Singhal, then posted with the ATS in Gujarat as its defacto head. Singhal was being probed for his role in the Ishrat Jahan 'fake' encounter. From what I had gathered during my research with my officer friends and journalists, he had isolated himself, had few friends, and did not entertain the media at all. I had been told that he was suspicious of almost everyone. How then could one approach him?

The email had details of Naresh and Hitu Kanodia, both popular actors in the Gujarati film industry. As a matter of fact, Naresh Kanodia was known as the Amitabh Bachchan of the Gujarati film industry. Hitu was his South Mumbai-educated son who had decided that it was wiser to follow in his father's footsteps than wait for a break in the Hindi film industry.

I was informed in the mail that the Kanodias were from the backward class and had a great rapport with many officials, including Singhal, who happened to be Dalit. Excited, I called up Naresh Kanodia who asked me to come and see him at the Gymkhana in Ahmedabad the following morning. When I met him he gave nothing away. He was absolutely expressionless while I spoke to him in my well-rehearsed accented English. He turned back to look at the mirror, took a swipe at his hair with a comb and then remarked nonchalantly, 'Ben, Hindi mein bolo na aur thoda aahista bolo, bahut fast ho tum.'

I had clearly not done my homework well. I spent the next hour explaining the subject of my film to him—the lesser known things about Gujarat is what I wanted to make a film on, I told him; for instance, the Gujarati film industry, and how those from the backward class had progressed in Gujarat. Now I began to see a flicker of interest in his eyes. For a man who considered himself a 'star', but whose success had faded in his home state with the popularity of Hindi films, an acknowledgement of his work from a 'vilayati' filmmaker seemed to finally have the desired effect.

The next day, I was to drive 100 km to a village where Kanodia wanted me to interview him and watch his stunts on a film set. As I went back to my room after meeting him, I sat in bed wondering about the futility of the exercise. The prospect at hand was high-risk but this was the only way. Armed with my SLR and notes, I stepped out of my room the next morning only to be stopped by Mike. 'Your lenses are missing.' I was still getting used to my new avatar.

The film set was constructed on the outskirts of the city in a village where thousands had gathered to witness the spectacle. Kanodia's son Hitu, a rather dapper South Mumbai grad, was dressed up as a prisoner while his father played the role of a cop.

I was given a chair to sit and watch the shooting. I went about my task diligently taking notes and photographs of the sequence. I was not the only one there, I noticed. A young man in his early 30s armed with a tripod and lenses was taking some stunning shots of the sequence. He was clearly not a part of the unit. He gave Mike and myself an indifferent look when Kanodia introduced him to us as a documentary photographer and went about working on his frames. The photographer was Ajay Panjwani (name changed) with whom I was to develop a strange camaraderie in the months to come; a friendship that I could never have had with my real identity, a friendship whose base was deceit, but Maithili needed that outlet.

The next few days went by with me visiting the Kanodias' set, engaging in conversation, discussing nuances of the film, while sipping the 'unit ka chai'.

Ajay who was a regular on the sets for his documentary on Gujarati films ultimately decided to be polite and in due course offered help if needed. It was on one of these visits to the film sets that I broached the subject of meeting some well-known cops in Gujarat, especially those from the backward castes. I told Kanodia that it would help if the official in concern held a sensitive position, one that involved bravado and had something to do with security in Gujarat vis-à-vis terrorism.

The last line had the required results. 'You should meet Mr Singhal, one of our finest, killed many terrorists.' I tried to conceal my excitement and went about noting down his name as if I had heard it for the first time.

'So what does Officer Singhal do, sir, where does he serve?' I asked with great show of naivete. This was all I needed from my filmy friends, an entry point, a reference that would not draw suspicion with the officers. The last person Singhal would doubt would be a filmmaker who had been recommended by one of the topmost regional filmmakers.

At around the same time, my source in Ahmedabad, whom I had briefed on the help that I needed, sent me another email. This had contact details of one of the city's most popular gynaecologists, who shall remain unnamed.

My uninor (mobile) network was not too kind on me every time I used it from the confines of my room. So most of the time I had to walk up to the terrace where inmates of the hostel would hang around for a chai or to light a cigarette. Mike was one of them. Later that day I called the gynaecologist from the terrace and introduced myself as a filmmaker who wanted to make a film on Gujarat and also wanted to capture the health sector in her film. The doctor seemed to be an affable individual, and asked me if I could drop in at his hospital the same evening. I was more than willing. Just as I was about to leave, Mike came running, 'Maithili, can I ask you something?' He said, 'Maithili, I can't work like this. You tell everyone we meet that you are making a film, but I am working with you, you should tell me the truth.' I tried to brush aside Mike's curiosity but now he was insistent, even hurt. 'I am not a child you know, I read a lot. I am on an exchange programme because I have achieved something in life. You should tell me. Do you trust me? Or for you am I just a foreign face you want to show around, more like an accessory?' I thought it was a very well-rehearsed line, but there was something about his outburst that persuaded me to take him into confidence about my real investigation. Before I left for my meeting, I forwarded him some links to my earlier stories. I asked him to read them so that by the time I returned that evening he would know the entire background to the current investigation.

My meeting with the doctor turned out to be extremely fruitful. He was more than eager to help. I asked him if I could meet a female doctor, someone who was very popular in Gujarat, somebody I could shoot for the film. I had anticipated the response; there was a reason I had made efforts to meet a gynaecologist after all. The 2002 Gujarat riots that had become a blot on the country's secular fabric had seen many agent provocateurs, and one of them was Maya Kodnani, an MLA from Ahmedabad who had been named in eyewitness accounts as one of the major instigators of riots in her constituency. Kodnani for me was an important character to explore, as I felt sure that she could help me go deeper into the story.

That evening the doctor called Maya Kodnani in my

presence suggesting that a filmmaker with an impressive profile from USA wanted to interview her and that he could personally vouch for my credentials. To keep my act going and to avoid any suspicion, I continued meeting the doctor once a week after that for what I would call my research work.

That evening when I returned to the hostel, Mike had jotted down several questions for me on a piece of paper, including names of those he thought were 'criminals'. Mike was right, there was a reason he had been chosen to be a part of the exchange programme. He listened to me with great concentration that evening, asking the right questions, grasping the right nuances. I told him about the plan of action and how I would be forced to modify it spontaneously if things didn't go as planned. How will we go about it, he asked. 'Tomorrow,' I told him, 'we have to sit for our first test.'

The next day we were to meet Maya Kodnani. As an investigative journalist I knew that information does not start flowing easily in the beginning and even if it does, one should not display too much curiosity. I briefed Mike accordingly. 'We have got to be filmmakers today, just filmmakers.' Mayaben's clinic was situated on the main road at Naroda. The Naroda Patiya massacre took place barely a stone's throw away from this three-time MLA's clinic, a massacre which saw more than a hundred people being brutally lynched. The allegation against her was that it was she who had led the mob that attacked Muslims while making provocative slogans.

Mike and I entered Kodnani's clinic where local women sat on narrow tables outside her cabin. At the entrance were two burly, well-built men, one of whom possessed a gun. Seeing me and Mike, he stopped us, cross-checked with his boss on the phone, and then let us in. He was Kodnani's bodyguard, who had manned her clinic ever since she had been nailed by the SIT. It was a two-storey building with clinics of various other doctors in it. Next to the clinic was an operation theatre.

On Thursdays the number of patients at the clinic, mostly from the lower income group, doubled. A display plate read, 'Only 50 rupees to be charged on Thursdays'. The compounder who eyed us suspiciously informed us that the clinic only catered to locals. I am a filmmaker, I told her, here to meet Madam.

I tried to scribble something in a notebook while Mike watched Sanskar channel on a TV set. An elderly lady who was waiting with her daughter-in-law, paid her obeisance to the 'baba' on TV by prostrating herself in front of the TV set. Mike looked at me with bewilderment. I grinned at him and turned back to my notebook.

At that moment, 'Maithili kaun che', asked Kodnani's assistant, as she stepped out of her cabin. She signalled for me and Mike to step in. I introduce myself and Mike with an accent. A warm handshake followed.

'You know, you have a beautiful name, it's the name of Sitaji,' said a visibly impressed Kodnani. 'Oh yes ma'am, my dad's a Sanskrit teacher so all of us at home have beautiful names.' That statement proved to be reassuring for Kodnani who much to Mike's irritation did not give him a second look. There were books on medicine and gyanaecology and some pamphlets of the BJP and some on the Sindhi community in Gujarat on Kodnani's desk. Next to these was a photograph of her son and daughter-in-law who are settled in the US. We discussed her career over the next hour, and she talked about her family as cold drinks arrived.

With reference to the fact that Mayaben was the Minister of Child Welfare and Health, I praised her commitment to the welfare of women in her state. 'So what do you want from me,' she asked finally. 'I just want to know more about you ma'am, we want to profile you for our film, as an achiever from Gujarat.' Nobody in their right mind, especially if they belong to the political tribe, hates to hear kind, flattering words and be part of something that glorifies them. We got an instant nod from her and an invite to her apartment for lunch the following Sunday. That would be perfect, I told her trying my best to roll my Rs.

Before leaving her cabin, I remembered to praise Ms Kodnani's saree and accessories. As we walked down the security personnel did not look very impressed. We hailed an auto and headed straight to Pakwaan. 'You noticed she was not even interested in talking to me,' said a visibly upset Mike. Before I could reply, the halwa and rabri arrived. When they serve the thali in Gujarat, they serve the dessert first. Mike's attention was diverted, Kodnani was forgotten, as the maharaj tried to help him pronounce the name of each preparation. It was a relief.

We returnrd to the hostel room at around ten in the night. As soon as I stepped into my room, I got an eerie feeling, something seemed out of place. I had carefully made my bed before leaving but now the bedsheet was crumpled, and my laptop was switched on. While the suitcase and drawers looked untouched, I felt someone else had been in my room that night. I was not surprised. I had actually anticipated something like this, which is why my laptop had been re-formatted before I entered Gujarat, and the admin name was set as Maithili Tyagi. On the desktop were files on filmmaking and research on Gujarat museums, the film industry and forests. Adorning the screen was a wallpaper of Lord Krishna. On the shelf next to my bed were books on filmmaking and photography. It was fairly clear that someone had frisked my room, and I was fairly sure that they had found nothing they weren't supposed to find. The games had only just begun.

The next morning there was to be a telecon with G.L.Singhal. There was a text on my phone from Ajay, the photographer friend, asking if I would be interested in a photography exhibition at Amdavad ni Gufa. I kept the phone aside. Mike knocked on my door. He was going for a walk across the Foundation and was checking if I wanted to join. December evenings in Gujarat can be very beautiful and chilly. The 2010 winter though was particularly harsh. To add to our misery, the hostel was located in an open, under-developed forested area.

At the hostel we only had the luxury of one blanket. When night came, most of us emptied our contents from the suitcase at night and tried to wear everything we could find—t-shirts, shirts, sweaters, jeans, everything that could keep us warm.

Mike and I wore an extra pair of jackets that evening and decided to walk along the edge of the forest by the Foundation building. I turned to look at Mike who was his usual thoughtful self. 'Am I doing fine Maithili?' he asked. 'Of course, you were very confident and don't bother about Mrs Kodnani, she was just too engrossed in the conversation and the words of praise,' I replied reassuringly.

That night before I went to bed, I sent a text to Ajay, 'See you at the exhibition tom.'

The next morning as I devoured the upma from the canteen I finally made that phone call to G.L.Singhal. Those days he was in the eye of the storm. The High Court-appointed Special Investigative Team (SIT) to look into the Ishrat Jahan encounter[1] was making headway in the probe and all eyes were on Singhal. He was the man who had shot Ishrat Jahan in an 'encounter' along with two other officers. A day after the encounter Gujarat top cop and chief of ATS D.G.Vanzara had called a press conference. It was a sensation, Ishrat's bloodsoaked body, along with

---

1   Ishrat Jahan, 19, was gunned down on 15 June 2004 along with three men she was with, by a group of policemen near Ahmedabad city in Gujarat. The local Ahmedabad police at the time alleged the group were a part of Lashkar-e-Taiba, a banned Pakistan-based terrorist organization, and involved in a plan to assassinate Gujarat's Chief Minister Narendra Modi. The other men killed were identified as Zeeshan Johar, Amjad Ali and Javed Shaikh.

those of three others, was lying on the road. She was named a woman fidayeen, the first of her kind in India, an LeT operative who was out to assassinate Narendra Modi, the Chief Minister of Gujarat.

Ishrat had become the talk of the town, narratives were written about Jihadist fundamentalism and how radical Muslim organizations were out to seek revenge for the 2002 riots. D.G.Vanzara was hailed as a hero, he had become an overnight sensation. Sharing the glory with him were other officers, N.K.Amin, Tarun Barot and the man who was of particular interest to me, Girish Singhal.

Ishrat's family in the meantime had petitioned the Supreme Court for an inquiry into the 'murder' of their daughter, Ishrat Jahan. A judicial committee was appointed by the Gujarat High Court and the verdict was given in 2008. The Justice Tamang Committee headed by an ex-magistrate of the Gujarat High Court gave a verdict that stunned the nation, 'Ishrat Jahan's was a fake encounter—the case needed further investigation'.

Human rights activists and lawyers came out on the streets to protest the gross misuse of power by officials to kill innocents following the verdict. The case lay stagnant till the family petitioned the Gujarat High Court for further investigation. It was then that a three-member bench was constituted to look into the encounter. Later in 2013, the CBI team appointed by the Gujarat High Court to look into the encounter called it fake, and listed top cops in the Gujarat police as accused officers.

It was thus in 2010, when the case was being investigated

by the SIT ordered by the Supreme Court to do so, that I
first sought an appointment with Singhal. The phone rang,
I introduced myself in my accented English. The response
was not very forthcoming. Singhal asked me to call him
later. All my hopes were pinned on this man. He was the
man I had to begin my investigations with. How would I
proceed, I wondered. The newspapers that morning had
spoken of Singhal's imminent arrest by the SIT. In a tense
situation like this it was only normal that Singhal would
concern himself with legal remedies rather than talking to
some foreign-returned filmmaker. I informed Mike that he
would not be needed for the day. Mike had become friendly
with fellow inmates of the hostel; one of them was a lovely
girl called Paarnanguak Lynge, a native of Greenland
whom we all called Paani. I suspected Mike was becoming
increasingly fond of her. Realising that he was not required
for work that day, he offered Paani a photography trip and
she readily agreed

I had my own photography trip that evening, I
remembered. Considering there was not much to do, I went
back to my room and began jotting down the events of the
last few days.

Ajay was busy playing host at his friend's exhibition
when I went there later that day. I was introduced to
everyone as a filmmaker from America. That was enough
for the lot to throw technical questions at me. 'Who is
doing your camera, what camera are you using, when
will you begin shooting?' I had rehearsed the responses
anticipating this line of questioning, and calmly answered

them. Ajay was visibly impressed. He showed me around Amdavad ni Gufa, and gave me a crash course on the history of that place before we settled for a cup of coffee and samosa.

There was a college group sitting next to us, somebody was strumming a guitar. Someone else in a distant corner was sitting with his date. For a moment it seemed that everything could be forgotten, the cops, that I was undercover, and that I was nervous about the task at hand. I was just another student. I thought of my family back home, parents whom I had not spoken to in days, who were anxious about my sudden change of behaviour. I had switched off my cell phone. I would communicate with them by dropping in a mail from a local cybercafé, but not nearly often enough. Ever since I had published the Amit Shah exposé, they were worried about my well-being all the time.

With such thoughts, I asked Ajay if he could drop me at a local market close to my hostel. I had some errands to run, I told him. He dropped me at the Satellite Road shopping area, one of the upmarket areas. To make the errand exercise look genuine, I walked into a supermarket, bought some toiletries and stepped into a PCO right next to the superstore. This was the safest mode of communication. I dialled our landline number. My mother, who has been a constant source of strength and had built a façade of being strong, took the call. She wanted me to come back. This was no journalism, when I had to be incommunicado with my own family. I reassured her as much as I could and hung up feeling desolate inside.

The next morning I called up Singhal again,and this time he said he would meet me. The harrowing journey that my investigation was going to take me on had finally begun.

CHAPTER 3

G.L.Singhal

Girish Singhal's eldest son Hardik committed suicide in 2012. Those close to him suggest it broke his father.

I met Singhal that morning in 2010 after our telephone conversation. Mike accompanied me after being throughly briefed about the sensitivity of the situation. Singhal was no ordinary man, he was in charge of the Gujarat ATS.

At this time, due to the SIT investigation, Singhal's moves were being monitored closely, and he was being cautious of the people he was meeting. His arrest was inevitable. The SIT was speeding up its inquiry. Two junior officers had already been arrested. Singhal could be the next. The charges against him and other officers included, among other things, conspiring, staging and killing an innocent girl in the name of terror.

The phenomenon was not new for Gujarat. There was an atmosphere of hostility that prevailed post riots. It was clear that the not-so-amicable relationship between the two communities had taken a turn for the worse. Narendra Modi was being seen as the Hindu leader who had saved the Gujarati Asmita from invasion. Both communities had suffered with the Godhra train burning and the carnage in Gujarat right after. Those who had come in the line of fire were bureaucrats and officers but nothing could be proved against them. Commissions of enquiry over the years have used the harshest words of criticism for the authorities and their actions, or inaction, at that time, but barring a few footsoldiers, most remained in positions of power. Perhaps emboldened by this, a slew of encounters took place in Gujarat, most of which were later to be labelled fake, by none less than the Supreme Court of India. Encounters which were a part of an effort to portray the danger ahead for Gujarati Asmita.

The trajectory of fake encounters in Gujarat has a sordid pattern. Samir Khan Pathan, Sadiq Jamal, Ishrat Jahan, Javed alias Pranesh Pillai, Sohrabuddin, Tulsi Ram Prajipati. These are just some encounter cases from Gujarat which are being monitored by the highest judicial bodies in the country. A brief look at the cases is enough to blow the lid off a saga of meticulously planned and executed murders. In one of my most exhaustive exposés in *Tehelka* in December 2011, I wrote,

> However, what makes the Gujarat fake encounters particularly disturbing is the cynical and false propaganda that was mounted around them. All those killed in these fake encounters were publicly billed as Lashkar-

e-Toiba (LeT) terrorists out to kill Chief Minister
Modi, then deputy PM LK Advani and ultra-Hindutva
firebrands such as Pravin Togadia and Jaideep Patel. In
the communally polarised aftermath of Gujarat 2002,
such false propaganda was like a match to tinder. It can
be no one's case that absolutely no Muslim boys were
involved in terror blasts in the country but to cynically
manufacture threats and bill petty criminals as 'terrorists'
only served to tar the entire Muslim community as anti-
national and helped consolidate Modi as the 'Hindu
Hriday Samrat' — a man not only capable of teaching
'Hindu enemies' a lesson, but one under constant threat
from jihadi groups.[2]

An earlier *Tehelka* story[3] had demonstrated that Sohrabbudin,
who was a petty criminal and an extortionist, was well known
to Shah before he was killed, and had raised uncomfortable
questions about why Sohrabuddin was bumped off and
billed as a terrorist. It is significant to remember that Shah
was not only the Home Minister at this time,and directly
responsible for the workings of the state police, but a
man who was so close to Modi that he held over a dozen
ministerial portfolios. Discredited police officer Vanzara, in
turn, was very close to Shah.

However, it was the cold-blooded killing of 19-year-old
Ishrat Jahan which had Singhal in the line of fire. His role

---

2   http://www.tehelka.com/2011/12/dead-man-talking/

3   http://www.tehelka.com/2010/07/breakthrough-expose-so-why-is-
     narendra-modi-protecting-amit-shah/)

in the other fake encounters only amounted to obfuscation in the course of investigation by the concerned body.

I first met Girish Singhal that morning as I reached his heavy security office with Mike in the Shahibaug area in Ahmedabad. Singhal's past laurels included the successful handling of the Akshardham attack which got him the state bravery award. It's very unlikely for an officer of G.L.Singhal's age to achieve the kind of recognition he did, but most in his department would vouch for it. The security guard at the ATS office was confused. A woman in a skirt sporting a bandana and a foreigner want to meet the ATS chief? A note was sent in to him.

Within minutes a constable walked up to the guard and whispered in Gujarati that we were some foreigner filmmaker guys who had come to meet sahib. There was a look of awe on the guard's face as Mike and I were escorted inside. Mike was his usual charming self. Any other 19-year-old would have been palpitating in the situation but not him. I was a little apprehensive about him though; did he completely understand the seriousness of the situation and the risk associated with it, I wondered. Any doubts I had in the matter were cleared as we entered the waiting room. We waited with a group of constables and senior police officials in civil clothes; the white, sturdy sports shoes distinguished them from the civilians. A television set played a Bollywood film which caught Mike's interest. It was a Govinda film which had some of the officials hooked while the rest went on with their routine work. One of the more curious ones came and sat next to Mike who greeted him with a polite

'Namaste'. In broken English, a conversation ensued which ranged from his love for their food to details of his foreign land. Mike was in complete control of the situation, with no evident nerves or over-enthusiasm whatsoever.

'Maithili Tyagi, aapko sahib bulaate hain,' said the orderly. Act One had begun.

Girish Singhal, a man in his early 40s, suave, well dressed, well mannered, held a half-smoked cigarette between his fingers as he asked us in. He was watching a video on his laptop. There were a couple of books by Osho on his table. 'Are you an Osho follower?' I asked even as I sat down, carefully placing my diary on the desk; my video recorder was attached to it. I had earlier decided that I would acquaint myself with my subjects before secretly recording their conversations. But Singhal was known to be a temperamental man. What if he said something significant and I did not have my recorder on me? And what if he refused to give me an appointment later?

I introduced Mike to Singhal, there was a brief acknowledgement and I turned to explain to him the reason for our visit in my fake accent. Singhal listened to me seriously, grasping each and every word I spoke, and nodding at intervals. Once I knew I had his attention, I attempted to drop some familiar names. 'Actually Mayaben was very impressed with you and thought you were one of the brightest officers in the state. We are also profiling her for our film.' It had the required affect. The grim, serious look on his face relaxed, he gave an acknowledging smile, and said, 'She is a very good lady, very spiritual.'

I thought it better not to focus on anything related to the controversies that he was surrounded by. A show of naivete and awe seemed to be the easier way to break the ice. He narrated stories of his childhood, his desire to fight the upper class, the Brahmanical attitude of his neighbours towards his Dalit family, and being the breadwinner for his family. Was joining the police force a source of redemption? 'Inequality breeds everywhere, even in this system which I am a part of,' he responded.'

What started off as an appointment for 15 minutes stretched to an hour. Mike continued to diligently take notes of details every time I asked him to, while Girish Singhal narrated stories about what had made him who he was.

From the shop owner who hit him with a cane when he tried to touch something at his shop (because of his low caste) to tales of bravado—of countering the terrorists who had entered the Akshardham temple. There was pride writ large on his face as he talked; he blushed when I complimented him on his achievements. At a time when everything around him was a troubling source of tension, when his very career seemed to be at risk, perhaps this acknowledgement from an outsider made him feel relaxed. We were served adrak chai while we soaked in the details of the mock drill.

The meeting opened doors for us. We were given another appointment the next week. But something else came up in the conversation that looked promising; when we were speaking about the caste system and specifically about those who managed to scale to the top in spite of belonging to the backward class, Singhal mentioned a man whom he called his mentor, Rajan Priyadarshi, the ex head of ATS Gujarat, for whom he had great respect. Priyadarshi, he informed us, also belonged to the OBC class and would help us shape our documentary and give it perspective. He had retired a year ago and lived in Ahmedabad with his family. Perhaps convinced of our intentions, he also offered to recommend us to 'Sir' so we could meet him easily.

After an hour of talking with Singhal, Mike and I stepped out of the heavily-manned ATS headquarters. We were both quiet, and nodded at the security guard on our way out who now offered us a smile and also hailed an auto for us. A kilometre into the drive, we looked at each other and smiled. 'It's going the right way, isn't it?' Mike asked. I nodded.

Over the next few days, we decided to give Singhal a break; hounding him with phone calls would only sound desperate and appear suspicious. In between I sent him a few texts to inform him of all the research we had done on him and just how impressed we were with his dedication and commitment to the state. The day of our next appointment arrived soon.

This time I decided to let Mike stay behind. I had learnt this lesson while interviewing politicians or having off-the-record conversations with officials. They were always comfortable with fewer people around and someone simply jotting down notes. As far as a record of the conversation was concerned, that day I was even better prepared than before. Singhal's attitude towards us in our previous meeting had emboldened me to believe that the next meeting could be revelational in nature. I was not disappointed.

That afternoon, I carefully unplugged my green custom-made kurta from the charging point. The upper part of the kurta, embellished in dark Kashmiri embroidery, camouflaged a tiny hole that was an inlet for the camera that was attached inside. There was a thin wire that went down further, which had a small button attached to it; I needed to switch this button on and off every time I had to record something. It was a tricky affair, there was a red light which went on every time one switched the camera button on. While I had practised it enough, there was always this apprehension that the light had not come on. To make sure I would allow my pen to roll down the desk and fall. While bending down to pick it up, I would quickly peep inside the kurta to check that the red light was indeed on.

That day as I stepped inside the headquarters, there was a familiar nod from the security guard, who took me for some sort of an NRI filmmaker—such was the impression the orderly had given of me to most officers—and a cheerful 'Madam shooting nahi karoge kya?' I nodded indicating I would begin work soon.

I entered Singhal's cabin that afternoon expecting in all honesty to be greeted with a pleasant hello. But from the look on his face, it was obvious that something was wrong. He was watching some footage that had been provided to him, it was a sting footage of some miscreants in his residential locality. For an officer of the level of the ATS incharge, this was hardly an issue. It was something else,

some officials from the police force were creating trouble
for him.

But then he cut it short. He went back to being his
typical cheerful self. He was curious about the research I
had done on him. He wanted to know if I had inquired
about him with others, and if I had received positive reports
about him. It was time for me to switch on to playing the
naïve girl from Los Angeles who had no inkling of the
situation back home, who was in awe of the man sitting in
front of her who had gunned down terrorists in one of the
most high-profile terror attacks on the country. 'You are so
brave. So I actually went about doing a google search on
the Akshardham attacks and whoa, it was stunning.' He lit
a cigarette and asked me to proceed with my questions. As
it unravelled, I got a glimpse into his rather troubled life.
The answers were mostly cryptic. But the long silence, the
studied gaze, the tapping of the fingers on the desk with a
troubled look spoke volumes. I had anticipated Singhal to
be careful with his thoughts and responses but it seemed
that imagining a rather harmless interviewer before him
made him want to talk that day.

I volunteered to meet him at his place along with his
family, his children, his wife. 'Oh please don't. They are
already troubled. They don't like what I do. They have
started to hate my job. When a police van comes home, I
ask them to park at a distance and not come anywhere close
to my doorstep.' Soon after he mentioned the encounters
which made it easy for me to transition to questioning
him about them. As I write this book, following his arrest,

Singhal has already confessed his role to the CBI. Not just this, he has also proved, in his statements and audio recordings of a taped conversation,[4] the complicity of many state government officials in the staged encounter of Ishrat Jahan. The Gujarat High Court-appointed CBI probe has in its chargesheet concluded that Ishrat was not an LeT operative and that the encounter was fake.

The chargesheet that has been presented to the court[5] takes into account the evidence given by Singhal to the CBI. It is important to note that the confession made by him and his arrest came soon after the untimely demise of his elder son Hardik about whom Singhal had spoken fondly when I first met him. Upset with the constant bad press his father received, his son committed suicide in 2013 and those close to Singhal suggest that it brought about a change of heart. The latest news from his front is that he has resigned from the police force and has refused to take back his resignation in spite of being prodded by the government to do so.

It is interesting that Singhal also told the CBI that he did not wish to turn approver or demand clemency but undergo a trial like most of the co-accused. It is difficult to read another's mind, and one can only surmise based on what one knows about the other person, but

4   http://www.tehelka.com/2013/07/tehelka-expose-validated-cbi-says-ishrat-jahan-encounter-fake/

5   http://www.outlookindia.com/newswire/story/ishrat-jahan-encounter-fake-cbi-chargesheet/802685

Singhal's strange request to the CBI takes me back to the conversations that took place between us in December 2010.

Excerpts from the recorded conversation with G.L.Singhal:

Q) There is so much that you cops in Gujarat have to take. Especially with the controversies?

A) It's a funny situation. If somebody comes to us with a complaint and we satisfy the complainant, we upset the government and if we please the government we upset the complainant, so what do we do, the police is caught.

Most of the officers involved in the encounters are from the lower caste. Most of them have been used and abandoned? By the political system.

A) Yes, all of them, in the police department, it's a powerful department.

Q) How have the riots affected the state? The police?

A) See, I have served in Gujarat during the riots and I have been here since 1991. So I have seen many riots. We have seen riots in 82, 83, 85, 87, and in 92 post Ayodhya.

Muslims were more dominant. In 2002, more Muslims were killed. See with Muslims it's like this. Especially in 2002 it was like this, Muslims were killing Hindus all these years so whatever happened in 2002 was a retaliation for all those years of being beaten by Muslims. And everybody across the world created havoc. They did not see the situation in which the Hindus were killed.

Q) I met Rajan Priyadarshi, the person you had asked
    me to speak to as a Dalit.

A) Oh, you know I have served in various positions and
    with almost all possible officers in the state. I am in
    the middle of the hierarchy so I think I've worked
    with everybody but I don't think I've ever come
    across somebody like him. He is the most upright
    officer. He is an officer who knows everything
    about policing.

Q) And he said the government wanted him to
    compromise but he never did?

A) Oh yes, he never did that, I know him.

Q) Is it really difficult to not compromise and still be
    a part of the system.

A) Once you compromise you have to compromise with
    everything, yourself, your thoughts, conscience.

Q) And is it difficult for an officer in Gujarat to live
    with his conscience?

A) Yes, yes.
    And when a senior officer who has an understanding
    of the law compromises, then it becomes difficult.

Q) That's what happened with you? How much did
    you have to fight ?

A) There are certain people who will try and put up a
    fight. There are those who will keep fighting till the
    time they die. Priyadarshi is one of them.

Q) What about you?

A) Even I have.

Q) But does the system support you?

A) No, not in the least. I am Dalit but I can do everything like a Brahmin. I know my religion, much more than them, but people do not realize this. If I am born in a Dalit family, is it my fault?

Q) And has it ever happened that in spite of serving them, when it comes to your promotions, you are not given it because of your caste?

A) Yes, many a times.
    See, it is rampant in many states and it is rampant in Gujarat. These Brahmins or Kshatriyas will not have a Dalit or an OBC as a junior.

Q) Is your senior a Dalit too?

A) No, but I am managing, I am indispensable for them, I have countered cases of terrorism for them. But yes they do their bit, at times they will send me to do a job that can be done by constables.

Q) Usha [Rada, more on her in Chapter 5] was telling me that you were also embroiled in some controversy?

A) In 2004, we had encountered four people. Two were Pakistanis, and two were from Mumbai. And among them one was a girl, her name was Ishrat, it's a very popular case. The High Court has directed to investigate what kind of encounter it was, fake or genuine.

Q) So, is it fake? And why are you in this?

A) Because I was there, in that encounter.

Q) But why are you in it?

A) See, all these human rights commissions it's all what they do.

    You know certain cases are difficult and you have to tackle them differently. Look at what America did post 9/11. There was a place called Guantanamo. They were kept there, detained, tortured. Magar theek hai na. Not everybody is tortured. There are 10 per cent who have been tortured and even if they have not committed anything, 1 per cent may be wrong. So this has to be done to save the nation, to save the country.

Q) So who were these people, Lashkar terrorists?

A) Haan.

Q) The girl also, Ishrat?

A) See, she was not but when she was killed in the same incident. I mean she could have been or not have been. Or she could have been used as a cover.

Q) I mean all of you Vanzara, Pandian, Amin, Parmar and most of the others are all lower caste. All worked at the behest of the state in whatever you did. So, it's like a use and abandon thing?

A) Oh yes, all of us. The government doesn't think this. They think we are used to being bound to their word and [ready to] fulfil their requirements. Every government servant, whatever he does works for the government. And then both the society and the government don't recognize you. What Vanzara has done, [but] nobody stood by him.

Q) But Sir, whatever you guys did, it was at the behest of the government, the political powers, so why don't they....?

A) System ke saath rehna hai to logon ko compromise karna padta hai.

Q) But Priyadarshi [his senior] was not close to the government?

A) He was close to the government, but every time they would ask him to do something wrong, he would refuse to do so.

Q) Yeah, he told me that they had asked him to do an encounter, including Mr Pandian. But he refused?

A) Pandian is also behind bars although I don't know much about his background.

Q) How did he get so close to the HM?

A) Yes, he was in the intelligence department before being in the ATS.

Q) See, I know that both the CM and HM are doing things for themselves? So are things easy for you now?

A) Certain things are not in our hands. We have done things for the system.

Q) Are you on the radar or is your case done?

A) The case is going on. Very much.

Q) So, is the state helping you or not?

A) See, whether it's the Congress or the BJP, political parties are political parties. They will first see their benefit, under what circumstances they can extract something. In our case they are helping, but also trying to see what they will get or not get, if it backfires then what will they gain from it.

A) Look at the people who are investigating our encounter, Karnail Singh who was the joint Commissioner of Police in Delhi for the Special Cell who has been transferred to Mizoram. During his tenure, 44 encounters took place. And he is now the chairman of our SIT. Then there is an officer called Satish Verma, who boasts of being a follower of human rights [but he] did some 10 encounters. He seems to suggest he is a clean one.

Q) What will be the logical end?

A) Let's see, nothing will come out.

Q) But you and a lot of other officers were also involved in the Sohrabuddin case right?

A) Yes.

Q) I met Geeta Johri.

A) Oh yes, she did a very good investigation and later Rajnish Rai. They did a good job. They arrested some 13 people by themselves.

Q) But what's with this Amit Shah thing. Also I hear about your officers... I mean there is some kind of officer-political group especially vis a vis encounters. I got this feeling as I got to meet a lot of other ministers.

A) See, even the CM. All the ministeries that are there and the ministers. They are rubber stamps. All decisions are taken by the CM. Whatever decisions all the ministers make, they have to take his permission.

Q) How does he manage to remain unscathed then, including your case, why has he not been indicted in the same case?

A) Because he does not come [as in, appear] in the picture directly. He gives orders to bureaucrats.

Q) By the same benchmark, if Amit Shah was arrested in your case, then the CM should also have been arrested?

A) Yes.

   In 2007, just after the officers were arrested for the Sohrabuddin encounters, Sonia Gandhi was here and she called the officers Maut Ke Saudagar. After that Modi, went out shouting at every meeting 'Maut ke saudagar? Sohrabuddin kaun tha, usko maara toh achcha hua ke nahi hua?' And after that he got a thumping majority. See, he got what he wanted.

Q) And the officers through which he got it done, he is not helping them now?

A) Nahi, they are all in jail.

Q) Did he ever question you about your encounters?

A) No, he never [did], dekho inko sabka benefit lena hota hai, riots hue muslims ko maara, benefit liya, ispar bhi kiya.

Q) But will your Shah Saheb now come back to the Home department?

A) No, he won't be able to, because CM ko usse dar lagta hai, kyunki woh home department mein bahut popular ho gaya tha. He knows the weakness of the government, so the CM will not want any HM to know everything and be there.

Q) So the CM and the HM do not see eye to eye now?

A) No, this CM, Modi jaise abhi aap bol rahe the, woh opportunist hai. Apna kaam nikaal liya, sab got his work done.

Q) His dirty work.

A) Haan.

Q) So how many encounters have you done, besides this one?

A) Hmm...around 10 shayad....

Q) All prominent ones, can I know?

A) No no.

The fact that the investigation into the fake encounters dominated headlines in the Gujarat edition of all dailies only created an alibi for me to ask probing questions of Singhal without arousing suspicion. As days went by and as I met Singhal, there was a sense of guilt, an empathy that I began to feel. Was he really an innocent man wronged by the system as he would have liked me to believe? He would give me instances or remind me of various characters from films to draw an analogy with his own situation, the conversation drifting to verses from the Bhagvad Gita and his dependence on religion. We would talk about Osho and even my smoking habits. 'Leave it if you can,' he suggested, 'not good.' He was developing a fond friendship with me. I was an outsider who was not there to judge him from an insider's perspective.

I could not really figure what this man was all about, and on one of the days when I returned to my hostel, I headed straight to the PCO. I felt terribly confused and decided I had to ask Amma. I was feeling sympathetic towards Singhal. I could not afford to do so. He did not have the brazen attitude of officers whom I had met earlier, who gloated about cold-blooded murders and encounters. But, there could be no justification for cold-blooded killings, if an individual was a part of it, or if he or she was an official who had decided to sleep over the truth. As my mother said to me that day there would be individuals who could give you many reasons for their behaviour, for their actions. All you have to do is go back and see what it was that they had actually done, and you would know if their justifications held any weight.

It was clear to me that by keeping quiet over the years, Singhal was as complicit in the crime as others, but one could not help but notice the brazen use of such vulnerable cops by the state administration. The use-and-abandon policy about which Singhal had spoken on the hidden camera that I carried cropped up years later when another top officer D.G. Vanzara complained of it. Vanzara, one of the topmost officers from the Modi dispensation who has been behind bars for his role in four fake encounters, reiterated in a letter[6] to the Gujarat state government everything Singhal had said about this. That officers like him were being used

---

6   http://timesofindia.indiatimes.com/india/DG-Vanzaras-letter-to-chief-secretary-Gujrat-government/articleshow/47201125.cms

to realize the ambitions of ministers like Amit Shah, and that the man whom he considered his God, Chief Minister Narendra Modi had betrayed him. Whether there is any political motive behind Vanzara's statement (who has since resigned from the state IPS) is something that will remain ambiguous. But the fact remains that many officers like him and Singhal had been used at the altar of what is now claimed as a terror-free state.

Singhal was not the aberration, he was the norm. This was something that I was to discover in the days to come, from his senior Rajan Priyadarshi as well as from a former police commissioner of the state and other bureaucrats. The hunt for the truth had only just begun.

CHAPTER 4

Rajan Priyadarshi

In corporate language there is a term called 'takeaway'—it refers to something profitable that one takes away after a conference, meeting or conversation. Rajan Priyadarshi was an accidental takeaway for me. It was divine intervention as one would say, going by the immense value-addition this retired cop made to my investigation. I must confess that I had never come across a cop by the name Rajan Priyadarshi till the moment his junior Girish Singhal spoke about him during our conversation. I had reported extensively from Gujarat and knew most police officers there, or so I believed. I had not met many, but news reports and interviews with the police fraternity ensured that I had enough information on the relevant ones.

It was surprising therefore when Singhal mentioned this name that I was entirely unfamiliar with. I had absolutely no research on him before I went to meet him. The only reason I did it was not to arouse any suspicion in Singhal's mind and to soothe his nerves about going about diligently as per his advice. It helped Singhal gain confidence in me that I was meeting other cops too, especially those who were non-controversial, who were not in the news. There was another interesting aspect about Rajan Priyadarshi. In an interview given to *Times of India* in June 2004, Priyadarshi, a 1980-batch IPS officer had said that despite being one of the high-ranking officials in the state he was still treated as an untouchable in his village. The *TOI* news report said,

> People from different walks of life often approach him with folded hands with numerous problems. But, when the same Priyardarshi decides to visit his native Kadagra village in Dehgam taluka, the equation changes dramatically.

> This senior cop still cannot buy a house in the locality inhabited by higher castes of the village. He continues to have a house in the 'Dalit vaas' of Kadagra. Though Priyadarshi does not want to speak on the subject, sources say that till last year even the village barber did not entertain Dalit customers.

Technically speaking this made my job much easier from the point of view of the film. Additionally, by the end of the investigation there was enough material to suggest that most of the officers being manipulated and mistreated by the administration were from the backward classes. But I had missed something very important. Rajan Priyadarshi was the Gujarat *ATS* Director-General in 2007 when the investigations into the fake encounters were undertaken by the Gujarat CID. Not just this, he also held a very significant posting as the IG of Rajkot during the 2002 riots.

And so Mike and I met Rajan Priyadarshi. I don't think we can ever forget our first meeting with this 60-something individual. He had a one-storey bungalow in one of the middle-class localities of Ahmedabad-Naroda Patiya. It was the same constituency where another of our subjects Mayaben Kodnani was an MLA. It was also the same area which saw the most gruesome communal riots and where the maximum casualties took place.

We had a tough time locating Priyadarshi's house; it was a rather unassuming location for an ex-ATS chief who had held some of the most significant postings across Gujarat for over 30 years. There was a government school and many chawls and nallahs that one had to cross to reach his residence. Not many were aware of his existence, but his next-door neighbours identified him as the policewala who had his own photograph framed and hung at the entrance of his house.

Priyadarshi was waiting anxiously for us, waving to us as our taxi entered his lane. 'Welcome', he cheered from the first floor of his residence. Both of us entered his house soaking in its rather unassuming details. There was a plaque right at the entrance which had details of the various postings Priyadarshi had held in his career. As we entered, a rather boisterous gentleman with the moustache of a village pehalwan and greying beard shook our hand. Two cotton shawls, pens and notebooks were handed to us.

What transpired in the next few minutes was hilarious.

Priyadarshi took an instant liking to Mike. The nimbu pani arrived. We had just about recovered from the shock of how generously we were being welcomed when a man in his early 30s entered the room with a 10-year-old boy. They were Priyadarshi's son and grandson and the latter was carrying a digital camera. 'It's not every day that we have foreign filmmakers at our place, it's our honour. One photograph please,' we were told.

When you are undercover the last thing you want to do is to be in the public eye or leave traces of your undercover existence. But refusing to let photographs be taken would not really have helped in this situation. Also a brief glance at the plaque with the chronology of his career graph suggested that Priyadarshi could be of help. Mike and I complied with his grandson's wishes and a couple of photographs were taken before we were escorted to the living room. There was a photograph of Priyadarshi with state and cabinet ministers and with the ex-Prime Minister Rajiv Gandhi in the living room.

'So you wish to frame our photographs, sir?' I asked cheekily, curious to know the purpose of the photos for which we had posed. We were informed that he published a local news supplement on a monthly basis and he circulated it for free to people he knew. That was a relief. We let go of that conversation with the assurance that he would use the photos only when we had introduced ourselves to all the subjects of the film in Gujarat. 'We would not want unwanted attention you know, sir, we would want to keep a low profile, 'I requested, and he courteously obliged.

The conversation was a monologue.

In a span of an hour we realized that Priyadarshi had given us enough material to write a brief for his biography. He was in every sense a character. The kind you catch a glimpse of in a film or a novel. But this meeting would help me with some very relevant insights into the manner in which the state machinery worked in Gujarat. He shocked us with details about the village barber who would refuse to cut his hair and therefore he had to build a house in the Dalit nivas, despite holding the position of IG, Border Range of Gujarat. The Dalit tag continued to haunt him. On many ocassions during his tenure in the Gujarat police force he was forced to do his seniors' dirty work. But he refused to take orders. 'It was very strange, you know it was like if you are a Dalit, anybody in the office can get away with saying anything. There was no dignity attached. I mean a Dalit officer can be asked to commit cold-blooded murder because he (apparently) has no self-respect, no ideals. Upper castes in the Gujarat police are the ones in (everyone's) good books.'

As our meeting progressed, Priyadarshi seemed to become increasingly anxious, but by then he had already said too much. During his third meeting with us, I went to see him alone. I had decided to rest Mike for the day so that he could go to Maya Kodnani's office for a recce for our shoot. It was something Mike had himself suggested. 'Should we not do something to make them believe that we are actual filmmakers?' Kodnani's staffmembers were more than happy to show him around. In the evening, there was a message from her: Did I want any specific location in the house and if we would be interested in a Sunday lunch made by her. I replied with a prompt 'yes'.

That day when I met Priyadarshi, he had sifted through copies of the newspaper he had published. 'You can take whatever you want from these. I think you have all the information about me now. When do you start shooting?' He was anxious, his body language made that clear. He had divulged a bit too much for his own good. Details of the time when he was posted as the State ATS head, of his clandestine meetings with the then Home Minister Amit Shah late at night at his bungalow and who once asked him to kill an accused in custody. Every time I met Rajan Priyadarshi, I felt I came back with more.

Q) Your CM Narendra Modi is very popular here, in Gujarat?

A) Yes, he fools everybody and people get fooled.

Q) In that case, as additional DG, you would have had a tough time working under them?

A) They never had the guts to force me to do anything illegal.

Q) Lawlessness is rampant here no? Hardly any officers who are upright?

A) There are very few of them. This man Narendra Modi has been responsible for the killing of Muslims across [the state].

Q) Achcha, I hear that the cops also toed the line of the government?

A) All of them, like this P.C.Pande, it all happened in their presence.

Q) Most of the officers say that they have been implicated wrongly?

A) What wrongly, they have done it which is why they are now going behind bars. They killed a young girl in an encounter.

Q) Really?

A) Haan, they called her a Lashkar terrorist. She was from Mumbra. The story created was she was a terrorist, who had come to Gujarat to kill Modi.

Q) And it's false?

A) Yes, it's false.

Q) And ever since I got here, everybody is talking of the Sohrabuddin encounter?

A) The entire country is talking of that encounter. They bumped off that Sohrabuddin and Tulsi Prajapati at the behest of the minister.

This minister Amit Shah, he never used to believe in human rights. He used to tell us that I don't believe in these human rights commissions. And now look at this, the courts have given him bail too.

Q) So, you never served under him?

A) I did, when I was the ATS chief. He transferred Vanzara and brought me [in]. And I am a person who believes in human rights. So this Shah calls me to his bungalow. Now I have never gone to anybody's bungalow. Nor anybody's residence or office. So I told him, Sir I haven't seen your bungalow and he was baffled and asked, why haven't you seen my bungalow. Then he said, Ok I will send you my private vehicle, come in that. So I said, Ok, you send me your vehicle. So when I reach he says. 'Achcha aapne ek bande ko arrest kiya hai na, jo abhi aaya hai ATS mein, usko maar daalne ka hai.'

I didn't react. And then he said, 'dekho maar daalo, aise aadmi ko jeene ka koi haq nahi hai.'

So I immediately came to my office and called a meeting of my juniors. I feared that Amit Shah would give them direct orders and get him killed. So I told them, see I have been given orders to kill him, but nobody is going to touch him, just interrogate him. I have been told, I am not doing it so you also are not supposed to do it.

Q) That was some bravado!

A) This Narendra Modi called me the day I was retiring. And then he said, 'So what are you planning to do now' and all those kind of questions. So I told him how I was stifled. Then he said, 'Achcha ye bataao, sarkaar ke khilaaf kaun kaun log hai, matlab kitne afsar sarkaar ke khilaaf hai.'

Then I asked Modi, 'Am I allowed to ask you something?' So he said, 'Ask.'

I asked, 'In the last two decades I have served in various capacities, did you hear of anything against me?' He replied saying I had been doing great work. Then I told him, 'Sir, in that case for the last 4 years, my ACRs have been termed as Excellent and Outstanding by my immediate seniors and Home Secretaries, then why did you downgrade them? Why was my performance downgraded by you?' I told him that I got all the information through RTI. He was stunned. He said, 'I don't call up my officers and HS?' I said that, 'Sir you don't have to call up the HS, you knew everything as the file came to you'

So basically I could have become the DG but he did not allow me to.

Q) So why isn't there any DG in your state?

A) Because Modi has to take revenge against an officer called Kuldeep Sharma.

Q) And I have been told that he has his own team of officers.

A) You know when I was IGP Rajkot, there were communal riots near Junagadh. I wrote FIRs against some people. The HM called me up and said, 'Rajanji where are you?' I said, 'Sir I am at Junagadh.' So he said, 'achcha write down three names, and arrest all these three.' I said, 'Sir these three are sitting with me and let me tell you Sir that they are all Muslims and because of them normalcy has been restored. And these are the people who have brought the Hindus and Muslims together with their efforts and brought the riots to an end.' So he said, 'dekho CM sahib ne kaha hai' and then this guy only was the CM, Narendra

Modi, [and he told me] that it was the CM's order.
I said, 'Sir I can't do it even if it's the CM's order
because these three are innocent.'

Q)   Who was the one talking to you on the phone.

A)   The Home Minister Gordhan Zadaphia.

Q)   When was this?

A) Around July 2002, so Zadaphia said he will himself
come.

Q)   And so who were these people?

A)   Arre, they were good people, Muslims, people who
were actually helping bring an end to the riots.
Anybody else in my place would have arrested
them.

Q)   And what about this Singhal? He was the one who
asked me to speak to you ?

A) I was his boss, he's now in the ATS. He was my
probationer, Dy.Sp.

Q)   So who all worked under him?

A)   Of those in jail for instance, Vanzara was under him.
So what they did was I was Border Range IG, so
they got me transferred because they had to bring
in Vanzara. So they downgraded the position to
accommodate him.

Q)   So is the police anti-Muslim here?

A)   No, actually these politicians are. So if an officer
does not listen to them they send them to a side
posting so what are they supposed to do.

Q)   The person who Amit Shah asked you to bump off,
was he a Muslim?

A) No, he wanted him to go because there was some pressure from the business lobby.

Q) In fact I was told that some officers had been forced to do the Ishrat Jahan encounter?

A) See, between you and me, at one time these people Vanzara and gang had arrested five sardars, and one of them was a constable. So Vanzara said that their encounter should be done because they were terrorists. Luckily Pandian was the SP then and he refused so those five [innocents] were saved.

Q) But the officers are not really anti-Muslim?

A) No, they are not, the politicians make them do this. If you are upright they will never let you be in a posting. Look at what they have done to Rajnish Rai and Rahul Sharma.

A) This government is communal and corrupt. Like this Amit Shah would come and boast to me about what he did to instigate riots in 1985. He would call everybody to his place, like in one meeting he called the Home Secretary and Chief Secretary and one MP and I too was called; I was serving as the IG [then]. So the MP told Amit Shah that you could not even transfer one constable. So Amit Shah turned to me and said, 'Why was this not done.' I had to retort that the constable had done nothing wrong. He was only stopping the BJP MP's son.

Q) But I am surprised he would tell you.

A) He would confide in me. In fact he was the one who told me about the Ishrat case. He said he had kept Ishrat in custody before they were killed and that all five of them were killed and there was no encounter. He would tell me, she was no terrorist.

Q) I am surprised he let you be in the ATS which was such a crucial position?

A) Haan, they thought I was their man and would do as told. So Shah told me, 'See, we have two pivotal positions vacant, the ATS and that of the Commissioner of Police and we need our men in both these positions. So we are making Ashish Bhatia, the CP and you the ATS chief.' He told me that see, we have trust in you that you will work as the state tells you. So I said if you really had the faith, why not make me the Commissioner of Police.

Look at P.C.Pande, he did not take any action against the rioters. He should be booked. He's in the good books of the CM. He's his blue eyed boy. He was responsible for the killing of Muslims. Hence you see, he has been given a position post retirement also. Although I have an excellent rapport with him, I know what he has done is wrong.

Some time in May 2013, my investigation of the Ishrat Jahan fake encounter case dropped a bombshell on the Gujarat dispensation. I had scooped one of the most crucial documents in the Ishrat Jahan and Sadiq Jamal fake encounters case. The investigation had the Ministry of Home Affairs in a tizzy. News channels went berserk. I was on every possible news channel explaining the details of the investigation. For the first time perhaps in the fake encounters case, a direct link had been established with intelligence officials; this time the mastermind seemed to be Rajinder Kumar, the Central IB official posted in Gujarat.

The exposé dominated headlines with the MHA on the backfoot and the CBI forced to question the IB officer, more importantly Rajinder Kumar, special IB director whose role in the Ishrat encounter had been established.[7] More recently Rajinder Kumar was in the news yet again after ex-Home Secretary G.K.Pillai, who had in his tenure stated that Ishrat was to be given the benefit of doubt, told the media early in 2016 that he had changed the affidavits at the behest of the Congress government in power. This led to Rajinder Kumar giving a series of TV interviews stating that he was being implicated. Questions have been asked about Pillai's dereliction of duty and the timing of his alleged 'truth' when he is now on the board of directors of the Adani group. Worse still none of them seem to have any remorse about the fact that irrespective of a person's credentials, an encounter was unconstitutional. None of them addressed why almost the entire Gujarat Home Department was caught on a sting tape by Singhal, talking of obfuscating the Ishrat Jahan investigation.

The crux of my exposé was laid bare in the first paragraph of my article which read.

The Central Bureau of Investigation (CBI) is set to

---

7 http://cbi.nic.in/newsarticles/pressclips/aug_2013/pc_20130802_4. pdf

drop a bombshell in a case of extrajudicial killing of four alleged terrorists by the Gujarat Police nine years ago. TEHELKA has learnt that the CBI will testify before a trial judge in Ahmedabad that one of the accused officers has, in a sworn testimony, identified Rajendra Kumar, now a Special Director with the Intelligence Bureau (IB), as a mastermind of the encounter killing of a woman and three men, all Muslims, on 15 June 2004. Explosively, a testimony by another officer claims that Kumar met the 19-year-old woman, Ishrat Jahan, while she was in illegal police custody before being killed. Another testimony by a cop claims that an AK-47 assault rifle, which the police said belonged to those killed, had actually been sourced from the Gujarat unit of the IB, to which Kumar belonged then, and planted on the four dead bodies . The CBI also possesses a secret audio recording made by a key accused, GL Singhal, who was one of the police officers who shot the four that fateful night. That recording of November 2011 is a conversation among Gujarat's then junior home minister, Praful Patel, who had succeeded Shah in the job a year earlier; Additional Principal Secretary Girish Chandra Murmu, an IAS officer who has served in Modi's office since 2008 and considered to be one of his closest advisers; the state government's most senior law officer, Advocate General Kamal Trivedi; his deputy, Additional Advocate General Tushar Mehta; an unnamed lawyer; and Singhal. (Patel, not to be confused with a namesake who is a Union minister, lost in the Assembly elections in December and did not find a place in Modi's new cabinet.)

It was as if the missing pieces of the jigsaw puzzle were beginning to emerge and fit together perfectly. Priyadarshi was the State ATS chief and Amit Shah had confided in him that Ishrat Jahan was being held in a bungalow, confined in custody before she was killed in cold blood. But like every investigation, I had to pay a price for this one too. There were stories linking my faith to my journalism. Within days I started getting calls from editors of various channels and lawyers that MHA officials had been slandering me by saying that there was a salacious CD of me with a CBI official.

I was stunned to hear this. I knew this was an attempt to silence me thinking that I would be intimidated for fear of character assassination. I went to my father who was till now blissfully unaware of what was happening. My brother Arif, a pillar of support to me, and my mom, the backbone of my determination, joined us when I called for them. My dad realized I was nervous and looked at my mother questioningly. She looked equally confused and nervous.

I told them all about the phone calls and the rumours which had been circulated. I distinctly remember my father's words, 'Dekho beta, ye sab drama hai, unko kaho cd dikhaayein, hum sab dekhenge.' He laughed; my mom started to breathe easy and carressed my hair. She said, 'Beta, hum sab jab tumko trust karte hain, jab tumhari family ne ek sawaal nahi poocha, toh tumhein kisi aur ki kya fikar.'

My brother, equally supportive, reacted like the senior

media-professional he is, 'Write a letter to them, lash out at these disgusting souls, is this all they could come up with?'

But I did not have to do much, my co-workers and colleagues from the journalism fraternity stood firmly behind me like a rock. Shoma Chaudhary who was then the Managing Editor wrote the editorial that week in response to the malicious campaign against me:

Senior Editor Rana Ayyub has been having a close taste of this in recent weeks. Over the past three years, Rana — one of TEHELKA's most sterling and fearless journalists — has doggedly chased the story of fake encounters in Gujarat. Her journalism has been driven by a keen sense of justice and constitutional values. Yet, as her scoops on the Ishrat Jahan case began to make national headlines, she has had to face the humiliating experience of being assessed not as a professional but as a 'Muslim journalist'. Equally dismaying, a despicable slander campaign has been unleashed against her — shadowy whispers about a CD involving her andCBI officers that have absolutely no basis in truth.

India is an imperfect experiment. But if we abandon the poetic idea that underpins it, this is what we will get: 'Hindu nationalists', 'Muslim journalists', and women professionals we try to defang with scurrilous lies.

The planted CD story died a silent death.

On the other hand, revelations were being made each day about Amit Shah's connivance with state cops to carry out surveillance against innocent civilians, one of them being being a young architect named Mansi Soni. It was evident that one of the key people at the centre of this was G.L.Singhal, once an Amit Shah confidante. The conversations were recorded at a significant time, when the SIT appointed to look into the Ishrat Jahan case had begun to make initial investigations into the case. Singhal, the officer concerned, who had begun to see through the state policy of using officers from backward classes, wanted to safeguard himself. And what better way to do it than use the methodology that was made rampant in Gujarat at that time—illegal phone tapping.

Data obtained through RTI by activists in Ahmedabad had stated that more than 65,000 numbers in the state were illegally been snooped upon—the list included members of the opposition, those in the party who were trying to rebel against the establishment, journalists and cops.

Singhal was no stranger to the mechanism and the dirty tricks which he had confided about to us. And so began the task of tapping the phone calls of the minister and his conversations. One of the most significant such tapped conversations recorded Shah's orders to Singhal to keep surveilling the activities of a young architect from Gujarat, Mansi, who had been introduced to him during the rehabilitation phase following the devastating Bhuj earthquake by an IAS officer called Pradip Sharma.

I had found out that Mansi was at this point living in Bangalore. I had all the facts of the surveillance on tape. But I was aware that publishing the tapes would mean that

Mansi's privacy and peaceful existence in Bangalore would come to an end.[8]

Time was running out. My editor Shoma would call me from her personal assistant's cell phone on a PCO number I had given her. 'What have we got?' she would ask, 'what's going on there.' I would give her the details of the transcripts and she would squeal with excitement. 'It's huge, Rana!' she would exclaim.

But for me, there were many loose ends which had to be tied together first. I needed to get in touch with some bureaucrats—home secretaries, principal advisors who were the ones responsible for signing various incriminating documents, and who would have taken direct orders from Modi and Shah. Most of them had been grilled by the Nanavati Commission where they had developed amnesia. Most were not complicit directly but by staying silent on any knowledge of wrongdoing they had become obfuscations in the due process of justice for the riot victims in Gujarat. It was easier for my colleague Ashish to get local goondas to speak about their bravado over killing Muslim women during the Gujarat riots. But I was looking at the key men responsible—the Home Secretary of Gujarat, the DG of Police, the Commissioner, and the Head of IB during the riots. My head was spinning each day.

---

8 Going by the indignity Mansi Soni had to suffer when the story later became public, and the pressure she was under from her family to relocate to USA, my fears were clearly not baseless. I ultimately decided not to publish my footage on this case.

As if this wasn't enough stress, Manik bhai asked us to vacate our rooms for an in-house conference because delegates would be occupying all rooms at the Foundation. I was without a roof again.

CHAPTER 5

In between

Before I can proceed to other characters of the story, it is important to introduce one of Gujarat's famous women cops, Usha Rada. I did not intend to sting her but there was an element of suspicion about her. I realized there would not be much harm in doing so since meeting Rada, who belonged to the backward class, would only strengthen the façade of my story. Rada was a junior of Abhay Chudasama and a loyal one at that. Soon after I left Gujarat, Usha Rada resigned from the Special Task Force formed by the Supreme Court to probe the 16 police encounters in Gujarat that took place between 2003 and 2006.

Already arrested by the CBI in the Sohrabuddin Sheikh fake encounter case, Chudasama had been Rada's boss between 2007 and 2010 when they were both posted in the crime branch. Speculations were rife that Rada would influence the course of investigation in favour of Chudasama.

The Gujarat police control room had become a favourite with me by this time. Every time I needed a contact of a police official I would call in a clipped accent and introduce myself as an American filmmaker making a documentary on powerful Gujarati women. The concerned police official who would be on the line would generously provide me with not just the landline but also the cell phone number of the relevant officer. When I called Usha Rada she was in the middle of an interrogation. I left her a text. Two hours later, she called back asking me to see her at the circuit house in Ahmedabad. I wore a denim skirt with a black t-shirt with loads of chunky jewellery for the meeting. There was a bandana around my head and I carried a camera and a slingback. The receptionist escorted me to the seating area.

Within minutes Rada arrived, a woman in her early 30s, with her hair in a boy cut and a tall, lean frame. She wore a collared t-shirt and jeans with sports shoes which added gravitas to her personality. She gave me a warm hug. 'Hello Maithili, how are you?' she asked with a warm handshake and a broad and generous smile.

Once seated I heaped praise on her personality; not all of it was untrue. Usha did have a pleasing personality, and a smile that would allay all my fears. Within an hour of our conversation she had promised to take me to the movies, shopping, and to one of Gujarat's most famous thali joint.

'Treat me like your friend and feel free to ask for any help', she told me before embracing me and dropping me off at the Nehru Foundation in her official jeep.

The next evening there was a message from Usha on my phone. 'Maithili, meet me at SG Highway at 9.30 pm.' I replied in the affirmative immediately but the moment I hung up I could feel anxiety rush through my body. Why would she want to meet me at SG Highway at 9.30 at night?

Feeling quite nervous, even fearful, I took an auto to SG Highway. The moment I reached the specified spot and called her, Usha asked me to hand the phone to the auto driver to let him know the exact location where he was supposed to take me. The driver grudgingly gave the phone to me complaining that I should have told him about the long journey ahead. It was close to 10 by then. I had no option but to heed Usha's request. If I was scared I could not show it. We drove for several kilometres before I saw Usha's police van on the road. There were only three other cops waiting by the van. I almost wanted to request the auto driver to take me away from there but it was too late. 'Hello!', Usha said walking towards me. She asked me to sit in her jeep. 'Let's go, I am taking you to a place you will like.'

I wanted to weep. For the first time during my stay in Gujarat my hands went cold as I sat in the jeep. Usha kept on talking while I was uncharacteristically silent. I wanted to pick up the phone and call my family. To inform them about the last person I had met, should I encounter an accident.

But I had misread Usha. We stopped at one of Ahmedabad's most hip restaurants. See, I wanted you to see that our Ahmedabad is no less than your America, she beamed. I smiled, a smile of relief which Usha would never understand. I excused myself a little later and made for the washroom. I don't think I would have ever wept as much as I did in that toilet cubicle. I was coughing, there was water streaming from my eyes, my nose, I almost vomited.

Before leaving the restaurant after a conversation that had her convinced about my admiration for her, we promised to meet the next day at her residence. At the restaurant the conversation veered from the Muslims who had been terrorizing Gujarat to her senior Abhay Chudasama being a hero of sorts.

The next evening I was to meet Usha at her residence. I unplugged my special kurta from its charging device. I checked the camera, wore the kurta, and left the Nehru Foundation. On my way down I was introduced to a new inmate at the foundation, Raji, a girl from Mumbai who was to be my next-door neighbor. Paani and her friends had just returned to the hostel. Another German girl had joined us at the hostel. She was chatting with her family on skype and asked me to say hello to her mom as I walked past her room.

By the time I reached the quarters for policemen near Shahibaug, Usha had changed into her casuals and the thali for dinner had been set. Her daughter was working on her laptop. She introduced me to her telling her to take tips from me about what colleges in US she should apply to following her school education. Usha was a single mother, she had divorced her husband and now lived with her parents and children. 'Aaj tumse tumhari police force ke baare mein notes leni hai,' I told Usha. 'Aaj nahi, aaj film dekhne jaate hain.' I was disappointed but did not allow it to show on my face.

Within minutes we reached a popular cinema hall in Ahmedabad. But the moment we entered the premises my heart sank. There was a frisking zone and a metal detector at the entrance. My kurta had a camera attached to it. This was it, I thought my mouth going dry with fear. We were in the queue. Usha chatted one to a thousand while my attention was focused on the barrier. Within minutes the detector would detect the camera and I would be caught, then and there. But miracles happen and it did that day when a constable standing close to the checking point saw Usha and me in the queue and escorted us from the other entrance. Even though it was December and very cold at night, I could feel sweat dripping down my back as I realized that I had been saved yet again. Loaded with popcorn and coke we entered to watch *No one killed Jessica*, ironically a movie based on a *Tehelka* investigation on the Jessica Lal murder case.

As the credits started rolling, the film acknowledged the work done by *Tehelka* and Usha whispered to me, 'Have you heard of *Tehelka*, these are a bunch of rascals. They move around with cameras attached to their phones and sting people. They did a sting of our people in Gujarat also.' Really? I asked with an extra effort at naivete 'What's Tehelka, some TV channel?' 'No no, it's a website, never watch it, all bad things about India,' Usha replied as we continued watching the film.

That night as I returned to my room I smiled at the circus I had become a part of. Smiled at the irony of the situation and the apprehension I had had earlier whether I would be able to live up to the expectations of my seniors. Would I be unable to unearth the truth? I also had two days to look for another place to stay. Paani offered to let me share her room but I could not take the risk. Every night I would charge my kurta, my diary and my watch, all of which had cameras attached to them. There was no way I could jeopardize my situation with the slightest mistake. I asked Paani for her laptop. I wanted to use my personal email which I had to avoid using from my own.

That night when I logged in as Rana Ayyub, there were at least a thousand mails waiting for me, many from friends who were curious about my disappearance. I had deleted my Facebook account so that there was nothing on the internet which could lead to a picture of Rana Ayyub. I immediately wrote a mail to a friend from the US who had family in Ahmedabad wondering if I could stay with any of her friends in the city as I was tired of staying in hotels.

She wrote back with an alacrity I did not expect. Her family and friends were in Rajkot but one of her family friends had a bungalow on SG Highway. The owners were not in the country and the house was looked after by a housekeeper who stayed in makeshift digs in the compound. With the logistics discussed, I packed my stuff and went to see Manik bhai in his cabin the next morning. I had to make the payment. You can come back 10 days later, he assured me. By then the delegation would have returned and a room could be made available.

The bungalow, although a beautiful structure with a huge garden and a lawn, was certainly not a place for a single woman to stay alone. To its left and right were bungalows under construction and makeshift slums where the construction workers resided with absolutely no light post sunset. There was no mode of communication and the caretaker used a bicycle to travel to the market which was about a kilometre away from the bungalow. There were broken wires, wood, bricks and mountains of cement in the premises. Kalu bhai, the caretaker was informed of my arrival and before he could open the main gate I was welcomed by two stray dogs. Kalu bhai had three daughters and the stray dogs were a part of the family and later would turn out to be my companions in solitude.

There was another surprise that awaited me at the house which Kalu bhai did not deem very important to tell me about. On one of the evenings when I returned to the bungalow in an auto, it was dark. There was no point knocking on the gate as Kalu bhai was in his little house with doors locked and the radio blaring. I called him on the phone and asked the driver to press the horn so somebody inside would hear me. I was carrying a portable torch with me to help find my way in the dark lane with no lights whatsoever.

As soon as I flicked the lights on inside the gate, the dogs started barking, I was glad because it would attract

Kalu bhai's attention. Sure enough, Kalu bhai called out loudly, 'Aa raha hoon Maithili ben'. The dogs carried on barking, however.

By the time I took a shower and ate my dinner, the dogs were still barking. I stepped out, and thinking they were hungry, I called out to Kalu bhai asking if he could feed them. 'Arre ben ek baar woh saanp hole mein chala jaawega na sab shaant ho jaayenge,' He replied. Saanp, I screamed, 'Kidhar??'

The next fifteen minutes Kalu bhai and his daughters exclaimed joyously about a cobra which had made the bungalow his home for the last one year. When they took me to find it, I saw the snake perching on the wall.

Since that day I could not sleep well at night. Every time the dogs would bark, I knew the snake was out of its resting place. I would often wake up apprehensive that somebody was trying to jump the fence. Something inexplicable had begun to happen to me. My pulse rate would suddenly accelerate, and I would break into cold sweat every night. My throat would go dry and I was finding it increasingly difficult to keep down any food. What if one of the officials discovered my true identity. This bungalow was the easiest place to cause me harm.

In the days to come when there was nothing much to do in the afternoons, Kalubhai's daughters would come to me with their school books. I would make tea and we would enjoy it with some Parle G. The dogs had grown very fond of me and I had reached the stage where I found the snake playing with the dogs entertaining. Kalubhai's daughters and I had named it Mukhia. The girls would hurl pebbles at Mukhia, while I would sit at a distance and shoot it all with my phone.

CHAPTER 6

Ashok Narayan

Mike was yet to return from Delhi. His family was visiting him in India and I had asked him to be discreet about his work in Gujarat. Around this time *Tehelka* put a testimony of Gujarat IPS officer Sanjiv Bhatt on its cover. The testimony was published by my colleague who was then Editor of Investigations, Ashish Khetan. According to Sanjiv Bhatt he was present in an alleged meeting[9] which took place between Modi, and the concerned police officers and bureaucrats, in which Modi gave them a free hand to kill Muslims during the riots in 2002. Most of the journalists, activists, and lawyers covering the Gujarat riots were perplexed. Many I knew and spoke to personally did not buy his argument, suggesting that no Chief Minister would jeopardize his political career by giving an order like that

---

9   http://www.tehelka.com/2011/04/gujarat-ex-intelligence-chief-blames-modi-for-gujarat-riots/

amidst dozens of top bureaucrats and officers. There were too many questions. Why did it take so long for Sanjiv Bhatt to come out and give this statement? In many years of reporting on Gujarat I had never ever come across Sanjiv Bhatt or any accounts by him.

Shoma called me and asked me if I could get the officers to speak about Sanjiv Bhatt. I was a bit wary of asking a question about this, an aspect so specific that it could arouse suspicion. I remember telling Shoma that somehow I could not bring myself to trust Sanjiv Bhatt's account for many technical reasons. I promised her that if indeed there was an iota of truth in his testimony, I would find it.

I wanted to meet the most important decision-makers during the Gujarat riots. There were four individuals who had been in key roles during the Gujarat riots. Home Secretary Ashok Narayan, DG of Police Chakravarthy, Commissioner of Police P.C.Pande, and Swarnakanta Verma who was the Principal Advisor to the CM during the riots in 2002. I had already started meeting Ashok Narayan.

According to the *Tehelka* report which carried Bhatt's testimony, most of the officials I have mentioned above had developed amnesia during their cross-examination by the Nanavati Commission.

According to the testimony of the 1988-batch IPS officer of Gujarat cadre, Sanjiv Bhatt 'had attended the meeting held by the then Chief Minister of Gujarat Mr. Modi who had asked the top police officials to let Hindus vent out their anger against the minority community'.

Later in October 2014, the Supreme Court quashed Sanjiv Bhatt's plea calling it an attempt to influence the court through politics and activism. The Court said:

> When he made such sensational disclosures after nine years, what prevented him from not disclosing the e-mails and keeping quiet is inexplicable conduct. In the statement before Justice Nanavati Commission also, he has failed to state about the e-mails. When he has sent the e-mails to the effect that his potential was not fully exploited by rival political party, what prevented him from stating about the e-mails before the Commission also is not understandable. The overall conduct of the petitioner does not inspire confidence.

In August 2015 Sanjiv Bhatt's services were terminated from the Indian police service by the Ministry of Home Affairs under the Modi regime. Sanjiv Bhatt has always remained a controversial figure with too many contradictions in his claims, concede his colleagues. It was most relevant then that Ashok Narayan be asked to answer this question among the other riddles of 2002.

When I met him, Ashok Narayan lived in a quaint bungalow with his wife in Gandhinagar. Yet again it was not very difficult to reach him courtesy the very efficient Gujarat Police control room. The meeting took place some time in late December in 2010. I had called him on his landline and told him about my documentary which would be an ode to the lives of the most important men in Gujarat. I told him that his credentials were very impressive and that I would love to meet him with my colleague.

The night before I had to leave for Ashok Narayan's residence I realized that I had exhausted my lens solution. At eight in the night when even getting hold of basic commodities was difficult, I could not think of getting lens solution from anywhere. I searched online for alternate solutions. A thread of discussion on some site suggested I soak my lens in salt water. The next morning right after my Parle G-tea regime I took the lenses out of the salt water bowl and put them on. My eyes started burning, and I realized I had made a bad situation worse. I asked Kalu bhai for ice cubes. With my eyes burning and red, I hailed a cab and gave the cabbie Narayan's house address. On my way I received a text from Ajay that he was in Gandhinagar and wanted to check if I was around. I was welcomed into the house by Narayan's wife, a pleasing personality who ensured I finished the namkeen which she had recently got from a well-known retailer. I was told Mr Narayan, an elderly gentleman in his 70s, was getting ready. Over two cups of chai, my family life was discussed, so was my ancestral home in Kanpur and the prospect of my marriage. She was a simple middle-class, educated woman who was enjoying a life of domesticity while her daughters lived abroad. She showed me pictures of her two daughters and offered to share their wedding album on the next visit.

Ashok Narayan entered the room with a warm hello and checked with me if his wife had been hospitable enough in his absence. Ashokji was old enough or perhaps older than my father, a spiritual man who believed in the concept of 'live and let live'. His knowledge of literature and mythology left me astounded. He was a poet too, he loved Urdu poetry and had authored two books himself.

I was the daughter of an Urdu writer who had won laurels for his work, and was raised amidst mehfils and mushairas at my residence. The urge to reply to Ashok Narayan in an Urdu couplet was strong but I had to refrain from doing so. Maithili was the daughter of a conservative Sanskrit teacher and had lived abroad. Also, Maithili was not particularly fond of Muslims as a community as part of her identity.

But Narayan did not betray any element of bigotry that was associated with the officials allegedly involved in the Gujarat riots. He was a liberal when it came to religion and that night he mailed me an ebook on spirituality when I told him about my frequent bouts of anxiety. In him I found a man who was respectful of other individuals, cultures and religion. All the more reason for me to have been optimistic about extracting information from him about the course of events during the Gujarat riots as well as the fake encounters. Which I eventually managed. He told me that as Home Secretary of Gujarat he had firmly stated that no permission would be given for any political rally, including the one planned by Pravin Togadia. He also said that he had been against the suspension of one of the finest officers of Gujarat, Rahul Sharma; he was suspended by the state under Narendra Modi soon after the riots.

These were conversations that spanned four days, mostly over tea, and on one occasion over lunch made by his wife. I was distraught the day the couple invited me to lunch. They had begun to treat me like their own kin. They often said that I had replaced their daughters' absence in their home. My heart wept silently as I heard about Ashok Narayan's lack of conviction in going all out against the tacit encouragement given to the Gujarat riots by the state administration under Narendra Modi. This was not my personal deduction. Ashok Narayan stated it in as many words.

On the day I was supposed to have lunch with the Narayan family I had asked for a couple of hours from the couple so I had enough at hand to profile them. I wore the favourite green kurta this time with a shawl draped around my arms, and my watch which had a dull fluorescent light every time the camera fitted in it started rolling. I also had my diary which had a camera stitched in. One never wants to take a chance with these meetings so multiple cameras were advised.

Lunch was ready by the time I reached. It was on that day that I began talking to him about his most crucial responsibility, that of being the Home Secretary of Gujarat. The ambience was just perfect, I had initiated the topic in a manner that looked like just another light conversation over food. Narayan spoke uninhibitedly.

By the time we sat down for post-lunch tea, he had started getting into the details of how Narendra Modi had handled the riots. I remarked, 'You know Mr Narayan, I have been doing a google search on you for the last one week and your name threw up so many links on Gujarat riots, Modi, the various commissions. It has been so intriguing for me and I am sure it must have been very difficult for you to deal with a man so controversial who almost bordered on the wrong during the Gujarat riots. For a person like you, so idealistic, so humane, I can only try to imagine what you must have gone through.'

And thus began the conversation.

Q) You must have gone red in the face when the CM asked you to go slow [while controlling the riots]?

A) He would never do that. He would also never write anything on paper. He had his people and through them the VHP and then through them [it would] trickle down through informal channels to the lower rung police inspectors.

Q   And then you were rendered helpless?

A) Precisely. And then we would say, 'oh why did this happen' but by then things would have already taken place.

Q) And there is no proof for enquiry commissions?

A) Several times ministers were standing on the roads and inciting crowds. One such incident happened when I was sitting in his room and we got a call. Then I told him a minister was doing this. So he recalled [him]. At least at that time he [Modi] recalled [someone].

Q) Was he a BJP minister?

A) Yes of course his own minister, a guy.

Q) There was a Maya Kodnani too, I hear she has turned quite anti-government.

A) She could have been there, yes.

Q) It was manic?

A) I will tell you something first hand. I know of a Muslim civil services officer, administrative officer. He called me and said Sir, save my life, my house is being surrounded. I called the Commissioner of Police.... he recorded or didn't but I think the man was saved. Next day the officer called and said, Sir yesterday somehow I was saved but it does not look likely today.

So again I called the commissioner and asked him to save him. After 15 days this officer walked into my cabin. He said Sir, it was the same story, in the colony Hindus were in a majority and Muslims were being killed. He said to me, 'When you rang up, the police force arrived and a minister was standing outside leading the crowd. The police officer saluted him. He saw the police officer and told them everything was fine. Later somehow one police officer recognized me and saved me.'

Q) But this minister is behind bars?

A) They are all out. But somebody has to do that. Unless somebody gives evidence how can you do that?

Q) Nobody has the guts to do that?

A) Nobody has the guts to do that.

Q) Who will take action against the ministers?

A) Let me tell you, I was the Vigilance Commissioner post the Home Secretary position. You know there is the Lokayukta in every state which looks after the ministers. So one day I go; now honestly AC kamron mein makkhiyan nahi hota, warna I could have used the word ki woh makkhiyan maar rahe the.

Q) So I asked what is happening?

A) They said sir, what to do. Nobody complains about ministers. When people are not willing to take on ministers in cases of bribery and corruption, how will they gather courage to [go] against ministers involved in riots. Kiski shaamat aayi hai.

Unless they come forward. And they are so smart they will make the conversations so smartly on the phone—they will call up the officers and say, 'Achcha take care of that area.'

Now a common meaning for a layman technically would be, 'Take care that riots don't take in that area' but the real meaning is 'take care that the riots take place in that area.'

They don't do things themselves, there are agents and agents and agents.

Achcha then you see that the FIRs are registered against mobs, so how will you arrest a mob?

Q) But haven't the commissions been helpful, those set up to look into the riots?

A) There was a Nanavati Commission, nothing has still come of it, they have still not been able to give any report.

When I was the Home Secretary I had given orders that nothing will happen unless written orders are given. So when the bandh call was given, the Chief Secretary Subbarao called me and said one leader

> from the VHP Pravin Togadia wants to hold a rally
> so what do you think. I said sir no such permission
> should be given because then things will go out of
> hand. The CM came to know of this. He said how
> can you say this. We have to give them permission.
> I said, Ok, then give me written orders, he [Modi]
> just stared at me.

Both Narendra Modi and Pravin Togadia were once
synonymous with the growth of Hindutva in Gujarat.
Narendra Modi (64) and Dr Pravin Togadia (58) used
to attend RSS shakhas together in the state. There is a
much-shared anecdote about the the duo travelling on a
motorcycle or scooter across Gujarat spreading the Sangh's
ideology. Togadia always rode the bike with Modi riding
pillion. Togadia was a cancer surgeon who joined the VHP
in 1983, and Modi, a full-time pracharak, was inducted into
the BJP in 1984. When Keshubhai Patel was Chief Minister,
both were in the core committee which took important
decisions for the government. When Keshubhai had to face
rebellion from Shankarsingh Vaghela who also imprisoned
Togadia, it was Modi who rallied behind him.

From 1995 to 2001 when Modi was almost exiled from
the state and became persona non grata in Gujarat, he would
spend most of his time in the VHP office as opposed to
the BJP office were he was no longer welcome. It has been
reported[10] that it was Advani who convinced Togadia to
bring Modi to Gujarat as Chief Minister in October 2001.

---

10 http://timesofindia.indiatimes.com/defaultinterstitial_as.cms

Togadia agreed to the change and got his right-hand man Gordhan Zadaphia inducted as Minister of State for Home in the Modi cabinet. Togadia had substantial say in postings of saffronized police officers, many of whom played a dubious role in the post-Godhra riots in February–March 2002 when the VHP and Bajrang Dal cadres unleashed a wave of terror in the state.

In recent public memory, Hardik Patel a young 21-year-old messiah of the Patel community has stalled the state over reservations. He unmasks a sword and asks a news reporter if he knows how many hands he has chopped off. It is believed that Hardik is a creation of Keshubhai Patel and Pravin Togadia who were later sidelined by Modi in Gujarat. Hardik, it is said[11] is a ploy to oust the powerful Anandiben, the current Chief Minister of Gujarat and one of Modi's closest aides. Anandiben is herself a Patel and now finds herself in the same situation as Keshubhai did before Modi's entry into Gujarat.

The 2002 Gujarat riots and the aftermath had Pravin Togadia provoking the Hindu masses with the VHP cadre running amok. In a speech delievered in Gujarat[12] Togadia said,

Terror was unleashed at Godhra station because this country follows Gandhi. We locked Gandhi away on February 28. Reform yourselves (Muslims) or we forget

11 http://blogs.timesofindia.indiatimes.com/masala-noodles/is-parveen-togadia-getting-back-at-narendra-modi-through-hardik-patel/

12 https://www.youtube.com/watch?v=f0HfmQY8aOw

Gandhi forever. Till we follow Gandhi's policy of non violence, till we continue to follow the practice of kneeling before Muslims, terrorism cannot be elevated. My brothers we have to abandon Gandhi. You know the Ramayana, it is relevant to the Godhra incident. At 7.45 am on Signal Falia the burnt S6 coach was Hanumanji's tail set on fire.

The audience claps, raises slogans of Jai Shri Ram. He then asks the crowd which is gathered at night in thousands

Who burnt the tail of Hanuman? Ravan burnt it. Hanumanji had gone for a walk, we hear Hanumanji had come to Godhra (crowd laughs and cheers). Hanumanji came to Halol, Kalol, Sardarpura and he stayed put in Karnavati (Ahmedabad) and didn't want to go back.

The reference was clear, Ravan was a term for Muslims. It was a clarion call to kill and butcher Muslims in Gujarat. While Togadia was doing the hard work, Modi was increasingly being perceived as the Hindu Hriday Samrat of the majority Hindu population which was constantly reminded that the Muslims were out to finish them off. However, this camaraderie came to an end days after Modi became CM. There was a fallout between the two. A report in the *TOI* put it rather succinctly:

The subsequent assembly elections in December 2002 saw Togadia address more than 100 rallies in support of the BJP, using a helicopter non-stop for almost two weeks. Things changed when Modi won the elections. He immediately dropped Zadaphia from his council of ministers, in a clear signal to Togadia that his interference in governance was no longer required. The process of consultation with Togadia and other Sangh Parivar outfits stopped.

Within days of meeting Ashok Narayan and gathering his taped bits on the Gujarat riots I told him that I would want to meet his friend and confidante from those days of rioting—Mr Chakravarthy, who was the DG of Police in Gujarat at that time. I was alerted to his role when Narayan and his wife kept saying how Narayan's only friend Chakravarthy made life less miserable for him in those terrible days. This at a time when most police officials had decided to compromise on their integrity to the Modi dispensation. The meetings and disclosures made by Chakravarthy will be discussed in the next chapter but while on Ashok Narayan it is important that I share with the reader the remaining conversations that took place with him. By this time, I had met Chakravarthy in Mumbai, and had wrapped my first meeting with him so my discussion about the Gujarat riots vis-a-vis other officers had become easier and less suspicious.

Q) Is Chakravarty such a controversial man?

A) See, he was the head of police, so whatever happened the blame would come on him and the home department. Even human rights department called it a constitutional favour so all of us came in it. Sanjeev Bhatt was in IB. Chakravarty was the DG then.

Q) So weren't you in the meeting?

A) Which meeting?

Q) Apparently a very controversial meeting in which the CM asked the officers and bureaucrats to go slow [in curtailing the riots].

A) Haan Haan, I was there in that meeting. I told you no.

Q) So you weren't called by the SIT.

A) Oh yes they did and grilled me.
Which is why Chakravarthy said that the meeting got them all stuck. Even Chakravarthy was a part of that meeting.

Q) Chakravarthy said that those who were close to the CM, some officers like P.C.Pande they were saved.

A) No, but PC got controversial later due to the SIT. I mean he also became controversial.

Q) But I hear he's close to the CM?

A) Yes, he is but this is what happened. If you decide to toe the line of the ruling party then you will not have any problem.

Q) And he's completely the CM's man?

A) Yes, and if he didn't then he would be thrown [away] like Chakravarthy.
Like they had to give me a retirement job as they had to supercede me because they wanted to make my junior the Chief Secretary.

Q) How shrewd!

A) So that's how I became Vigilance Commissioner
[his wife adds]: Not just him, but three other officers like him were superceded.

Q) Like that Sreekumar you spoke about?

A) Yes, he will give a lot of masala for your film, mostly sensationalism but mixed with truth. The funniest part is Sreekumar was on a side posting during the riots and post riots he was asked to join in and that too at my and Chakravarthy's recommendation. He had CBI experience.

But later he started filing affidavits at times of events which he was not privy to and so he too was later superceded. In fact the CM wanted to suspend him. We asked him not to. It looked like he was working more for the press. Leaking out stuff to the press.

Q) But why has the CM been so much in the line of fire? Is it because he's with the BJP?

A) No, because he supported the VHP during the time of the riots. He did it to get Hindu votes which he did. He did what he wanted to do and that happened.

Q) But he asked people to go slow?

A) He would not say that in the meeting. He would say that to his men. He would convey to the VHP and then to officers like Tandon and other officers and the VHP. And as an officer you can choose to toe the line.

Q) Chakravarthy did not toe the line?

A) We two were the only people. We did our job.
I told them, when I joined the forces it was to serve the people, not to serve the ruling party.

Q) Why didn't the others do that then?

A) Because they had to play the game, they had a goal, you have to compromise.

Look at people like Chakravarthy, they haven't got promotions, not sent abroad, but he did what his conscience said.

Q) How did the people outside know of this controversial meeting?

A) There was this minister here, Haren Pandya, he was the first one to say in the press.

Q) Who all were in the meeting?

A) CS, ACS, Home Secretary, DGP, officers.

Even for a layperson the above conversation would reveal the level of complicity of the state administration during the Gujarat riots. What Ashok Narayan was telling me was something most of us knew but it had never been said by an official figure, the man on whom most eyes were fixed during the Gujarat riots. What is more revealing is the sociological and political context the ex-Home Secretary talked of when he spoke about the Gujarat riots and what it meant for Narendra Modi. That he is objective can be ascertained from the fact that at no point does he try to mix facts with fiction. He even expresses his apprehensions about the manner in which Sreekumar leaked his affidavits to the media. He further talks of a meeting which took place in Gandhinagar during the Gujarat riots but at no point suggests that the CM gave marching orders against Muslims. Rather he makes a more nuanced argument about how these orders were given personally to officers who found favour with the dispensation.

I sat there listening to this gentle, unassuming man as he said things to me that he had not even stated during his cross-examination by the Nanavati Commission.

A) VHP at the behest of BJP called the bandh and that's how it began.

Q) That was a big problem for you to handle?

A) Yes, unless the signal went from the BJP it was difficult to handle.

Q) What is Modi's reputation?

A) He is worshipped, orthodox Hindus believe he holds the flag.

Q) Wasn't his role partisan?

A) He could have apologized for the Godhra incident, he could have apologized for the riots.

Q) I have been told that Modi did play a partisan role though, that of instigating, like bringing the bodies from Godhra and dilly-dallying on decisions.

A) I had given a statement that he is the one who had made the decision of bringing the bodies to Ahmedabad.

Q) Then the state must have been up against you?

A) See, bringing the bodies to Ahmedabad flared up the whole thing but he was the one who took the decision.

As we were talking, Ashok Narayan had a surprise visitor—Kailashnathan, a man known to be closest to Narendra Modi and his Principal Advisor then. Kailashnathan had dropped in after Ashok Narayan had left a message at the CM's office that his brother-in-law wanted to contest the assembly elections from Himachal Pradesh which were due soon. Modi who had been a former in-charge of Himachal Pradesh before he was sent to Gujarat still enjoyed a great deal of clout in the state.

There was something very discomfiting here. Was this the reason why officers refused to go all out against Narendra Modi? Because of this careful generosity? It made me uncomfortable.

After Kailashnathan left, Ashok Narayan's wife told me how important he was and that I should seek his help should I ever face any difficulty in making the film.

The conversation with Narayan continued after the Principal Advisor left.

Q) What has been the most challenging part of your job

A) I always felt bad that so many people were killed during the riots. For instance, many journalists asked why we hadn't resigned?
I had told them that if I felt guilty I would.

Q) But they weren't wrong, you were caught in a politically volatile situation....

A) No state government has to face such riots. We had only four companies for [controlling the] riots. Even CRPF is not competent but we would have been happy to have even one team. And the government at the centre too was the BJP.

Q) So the CM could have easily asked for more troops? Was it like a liaison between the centre and the state?

A) Of course liaison was there. Our CM could talk to Mr Advani any time he wanted to.

Q) I have been told they are good friends?

A) Very good friends, yes, so this was one factor.

Q) No forces. Didn't you tell the CM?

A) He knew everything. You think he was not aware? Secondly, the Hindu community, their behaviour really shocked me...looting houses shamefully, they used to come in cars and loot...humans at their worst.

Q) What led them?

A) The Godhra incident.

Q) Must have been quite a turmoil...reporting to the same people.

A) They never had the guts to tell me to do anything wrong.

Q) Was the government's ire directed against you?

A) Yes of course, I said give me the orders on paper, whatever it is.

See all the officers at lower levels, everybody has the right to arrest those politicians indulging in such crimes but most of them have come under political pressure and compromised.

Q) That's what happened during the riots?

A) Yes, in this era of mobile phones, you don't need to give orders on papers, you just need to call.

Q) The CM would have hated you?

A) Not too sure if he hated me, but he would have surely wished there was somebody else in my place.

Q) How did they all converge, how did the riots take place?

A) It was all planned by the VHP. It was gruesome, both Godhra and the riots and none could be justified.

Q) The riots were a reaction to the train burning?

A) You can't justify A with B.

Q) The CM should have stepped down. He was the chief minister, especially after so much has happened.

A) At one stage he was going to be changed, in the Goa meeting. Apparently he resigned but under Advani's pressure, Advani pressurized Vajpayee to not accept the resignation. I had given a presentation about the riots to then PM Vajpayee and Modi was also there.

Q) The CM would not have been very happy with that?

A) It was not a question of being happy or unhappy. I had to give a presentation of what happened. At that time also I could see that Vajpayee was unhappy with Modi and his role.

Q) He also surely went slow? He could have showed alacrity? He played politics.

A) He would have gained had he stepped down then, as in politically. Now he's trying to get rid of that image.

Q) He came to power on the basis of religion? His rhetoric....

A) In 2002 he got his votes because of the riots ...he

got more votes in 2007 because he built an image of development.

Q) How were the others, the officers?

A) Frankly speaking as the ex-Secretary, the DGP was himself a man of integrity, but he was too mild to be an effective police officer. He didn't bow to political diktats during the riots but he could not control his men, his police officers. Otherwise he was upright. Supposing some pressures were there from the government to transfer officers, he would say no, get me orders on paper.

Q) He must have then been in the bad books of the government?

A) Yes, he was. A good thing for me was that he was there with me during the riots, at least one impartial man. So that was a good support.

Technically all the cabinest minister have all the powers except for specific powers like collectors and DMs do. All other powers, though there is a delegation. But if cabinet ministers give you illegal orders than the Constitution of India gives you the permission to say No.

Q) Did you have the guts during that time [riots] to say no?

A) We had to say what we had to say. All said and done they don't have the guts to give such orders, they don't have on paper. So I said I will act upon what the papers tell me.

Q) You must have faced the ire of the state government?

A) I did. I was not given the post of Chief Secretary. But the officers like inspectors and darogas had the power to arrest a minister including the CM. But they chose to side with the government.

Q) Is this what happened?

A) Yes and in this era of mobile phones, they just tell them to do the job. And the officers care more for promotions.

When the army came in they needed a lot of paraphernalia.

As a matter of fact we did not get proper force meant for riots. All the forces were in Ayodhya. Central government didn't give [them to] us.

Q) How political did the riots get?

A) They were communally charged. The ruling party supported the bandh [call] given by the VHP. That was a big problem and the senior police officers would tell us that unless the political signal goes from the BJP it won't work. Because they think we are siding with the people.

Q) But Modi [Modi's victory] looks to be more a work of PR than anything else?

A) Absolutely.

Q) Look at the entire hype around Vibrant Gujarat.

A) [He nods].

Q) But why is he targeted so much?

A) He is being targeted because he chose to support the VHP. He did precisely what he had to do and he got what he wanted.

People like Chakravarthy didn't get praised, didn't get rewards, [because] they chose to listen to their conscience.

Q) Everybody is really praising G.Subbarao, the Chief Secretary?

A) Really?

Q) I am being sarcastic.

A) Unfortunately Subbarao wanted to please the government, he wanted to please the CM, but he could not succeed even with that [smiles].

Q) Why?

A) I mean he was given a comfortable five-year tenure by the government post his retirement.

Q) How much should I be mentioning about the riots in my film?

A) See, then your film will get controversial. Because the riots were controversial.

Q) So, I did not ask your CM a single question about the riots?

A) If you had, he would have diverted you and of course not given you a second meeting.

Q) Why did a man like Bhatt go against the CM and the government?

A) There must have been a reason. Whoever his boss is must have told him. It must have been at the instance of whoever was bossing over him.

Q) How credible is he?

A) He's not credible

Q) Achcha by the way, Jayanti Ravi's reference was given to me by Maya Kodnani.

A) Oh achcha....

Q) She sounded very anti-government?

A) Now she is, but earlier she was not. Earlier she was with the CM, the government.

Q) She was upset with the fact that nobody came to her rescue?

A) Political bosses never come to anybody's rescue.

Q) She claims to be all innocent.

A) In the riots she was definitely pro-RSS, pro-CM, pro-VHP.

Q) Which means she actively participated during the riots?

A) Yes.

Q) How is Rahul Sharma?

A) He's one of the rebels.

Q) As in?

A) Well, he didn't help anybody. He just wanted to control the riots.

Q) Was he also thrown out?

A) He was transferred out. In spite of the DGP's recommendation, Mr Chakravarthy's recommendation and my supporting his recommendation.

Q) Just because he went against the CM?

A) Definitely.

It is here that one needs to tell the story of officer Rahul Sharma whom I briefly met on two or three social occasions.

The first time I met Rahul was when he had come to see a lawyer friend with his very educated and dignified wife. Sharma struck me as a quiet man who was not in the habit of narrating stories of his bravado to journalists. He let his work speak for itself and chose to remain silent on his legal case till such time that I was around. He was being hounded by the state government at that time—he was superceded, given negative remarks in his annual confidential report, and two departmental chargesheets were issued against him. The Gujarat government subsequently cleared his request for premature retirement in 2015.

An *Indian Express* report of February 2015 said this about him:

> Sharma was among the officers who took on the state government in the 2002 Godhra riot cases and collected critical evidence as an investigator in the Naroda Patiya, Naroda Gaam and Gulberg Society massacre cases while assisting the probe in 2002. Even as he is fighting a legal battle in the Central Administrative Tribunal on three counts — negative remarks in his Annual Confidential Report, and two departmental chargesheets issued to him — he had applied for retirement three months back, picking February 28, 2015, as the D-day. The state government, however, took a call on his letter only two days before his requested date.[13]

---

13 http://indianexpress.com/article/india/india-others/gujarat-ips-officer-rahul-sharma-who-took-on-govt-to-retire/

However to understand the government's ire against Rahul Sharma it is also essential to know what the Supreme Court-appointed SIT thought of his persecution. A key point of the SIT report on the 2002 riots was that it affirmed that the Narendra Modi government persecuted police officers who tried to put an end to the violence in 2002 and that their persecution and hounding by the state had continued even after the riots.

The Gujarat government had issued a notice to senior IPS officer Rahul Sharma asking how and why he submitted phone records of senior politicians and bureaucrats during the riots to inquiry commissions without approval. In its notice, nine years after the riots, it asked Sharma why action should not be taken against him.

This came at a time when the SIT itself stated that the Modi government did not keep any records or minutes of the crucial meetings it held during the riots.

Sharma, a 1992 batch IPS officer was DCP (control room), Ahmedabad, in April 2002. Investigating the violence at Naroda Patiya and Gulberg Society, he collected data from AT&T and CelForce mobile service providers of all calls received and made in Ahmedabad during this period and handed over these to the Crime Branch. These CDs containing phone records of senior ministers, police officers, and members of RSS and VHP to each other were subsequently 'lost'. But while deposing before the Nanavati Commission set up in March 2002 to inquire into the riots, Sharma submitted a copy of this CD that he had preserved.[14]

My colleague Anumeha Yadav wrote a report in *Tehelka* which said:

These phone records have been one of the most significant pieces of evidence in nailing the guilty, including the arrest and the cancelling of anticipatory bails of Gujarat VHP president Jaideep Patel and minister Maya Kodnani in 2009, and in the investigation into the killing of Congress ex-MP Ahsan Jafri and 30 others at Gulberg Society. The CDs are vital pieces of evidence in the Naroda Patiya violence in which 105 Muslims were killed by official count.

But scuttling any effort for fair investigations seems to be the norm in Gujarat. A week before Sharma received his notice, another senior IPS officer, Satish Verma, member of a separate SIT set up to inquire into the 2004 Ishrat Jehan encounter, flagged that he was being restricted from pursuing leads in the case. Verma, one of three police officers probing this encounter allegedly carried by Gujarat police officers to please their political bosses, even submitted an affidavit citing instances of interference.

In an 80-page affidavit in the Gujarat High Court on 28 January, Verma described how obvious forensic evidence had been ignored by a previous SIT set up by the Gujarat

---

14 Ibid.

government in 2009, including bullets in Ishrat's body that did not match the weapons the police claim were used in the encounter. Verma described how Mohan Jha, a Gujarat cadre officer, who was also a member of the previous SIT, and Karnail Singh, a Delhi cadre officer, deliberately forwarded the retraction of a key witness to the HC without any comments to create doubt and ambiguity. Verma disclosed how Jha, who is the current JCP, Detection of Crime Branch (DCB), tried to put 26 police officers directly under himself in the Special Operations Group last month, claiming they were needed for security in the Vibrant Gujarat summit. All 26 were with the DCB on the day of the encounter.

'Verma says he had started maintaining an official note on what is going on in the SIT in December, 19 days after the SIT began work. This shows he saw the need to put the irregularities on the record and anticipated that his efforts for a fair investigation would be obstructed. It shows how twisted this attempt to investigate these fake encounter killings is,' says a senior police officer, requesting anonymity.[15]

Ashok Narayan was eloquent as he spoke about the fake encounters that followed the riots.

Q) What about the encounters?

A) Encounters are less on religious lines than political.

---

15 http://www.tehelka.com/2011/02/senior-ips-officer-sanjeev-bhatt-arrested-in-ahmedabad/?singlepage=1

Look at the Sohrabuddin encounter. He was killed at the behest of politicians. Amit Shah is behind bars because of that.

Everywhere it is happening. It's happening here also. Fake encounters are either politically motivated or [due to] over-enthusiasm of cops.

Q) Not during your term as Home Secretary?

A) Not the Sohrabuddin [encounter]. Just one of them.

I told the officers, what they were doing... must be politically motivated. I told the DGP, 'what are you people doing?'

Q) You should write a book on what really happened during the riots?

A) But who will believe me?

Q) You were the Home Secretary.

A) The Congress people will say you were a part of the government, [so] 'he has written [the] government version.' The BJP will not agree with my version [either]. Political parties will believe what they want to.

This was one of my last meetings with Ashok Narayan. He confirmed almost everything that I had heard in off-the-record conversations with officials over the years. That some government officials who chose to side with the government were awarded, others were superceded. Let us assume for the sake of argument that Ashok Narayan was being judgemental and opinionated. Even then the transfers and vindictive attitude of the Modi government towards officers who went against the administration is there for all to see. Rahul Sharma, Rajnish Rai, Satish Verma, Kuldip Sharma, all these officers have had at least 20-year-old innocuous cases unearthed and used against them. These were officers who had tried to keep the flag of justice flying high at a time when justice was at its lowest ebb in Gujarat, and for that they are being persecuted till today.

We will see in later chapters how Kuldip Sharma, the man who was to be the DG of Gujarat was denied his promotion simply because he started an investigation against then Home Minister Amit Shah in the Madhopura Cooperatives case. SP Rahul Sharma was suspended and had cases slapped against him for preventing rioters in a madrassa and later for providing the call records of various ministers during the Gujarat riots to the investigating commissions. The dust had just about begun to clear. Ashok Narayan had confirmed the bias and complicity of a state where blood was allowed to flow in one of the deadliest riots that spanned a period of three months.

It was time to move to the next character and the next chapter

CHAPTER 7

G.C.Raigar

I met G.C. Raigar, Intelligence Head of Gujarat during the 2002 riots and later DG of Police during the Sohrabuddin encounter, on a day when everyone was excited about the scheduled India-Pakistan cricket match. Ajay had arranged a screening at his place to be attended by most of his friends and had even invited me. I would have loved to go but did not in order to avoid exposing myself to Ajay's friends, many of whom had strong political connections. He had revealed to me earlier that one of his close friends was Anar Patel who ran an NGO in the city. Anar is the daughter of the Chief Minister of Gujarat, Anandiben Patel.

When I arrived to meet Raigar that afternoon, he was anxiously waiting for the match to start. 'I hope Afridi does not start hitting sixes, sir; as it is our bowling line-up isn't very strong,' I shared my two bits. Raigar served Rajasthani Chivda and tea and began reminiscing about his days as the head of the Gujarat IB. He had appeared before the CBI in the Sohrabuddin fake encounters case and was under tremendous pressure at that point, as per newspaper reports.[16]

This was one meeting I was extremely apprehensive about as I had absolutely no idea on which side of the fence Raigar stood, and how much truth one could elicit from him. Mike was back, and we had shifted back to the Nehru Foundation yet again. We met Raigar at his office where he had been given a post-retirement job of looking into cases of spurious liquor. R.B.Sreekumar ADGP, Intelligence during the 2002 Gujarat riots had stated in an interview after the riots:

> Many officials, in order to keep people at the top happy, did not do anything. Even my predecessor GC Raigar backed out. Subsequently, he was rewarded with a promotion even though he was my junior. He's even been given a post retirement as a member of the Spurious Liquor Commission, which comes under a high court judge.

Raigar, who was named by Bhatt in his affidavit to the Supreme Court, refused to confirm or deny if Bhatt had indeed attended the Chief Minister's meeting on 27 February 2002. 'I can't say anything, I was on leave that day,' he had told a local newspaper.

---

16 http://epaper.timesofindia.com/Default/Layout/Includes/
MIRRORNEW/ArtWin.asp?
From=Archive&Source=Page&Skin=MIRRORNEW&BaseHref=
PMIR%2F2010%2F07%2F27&ViewMode=HTML&PageLabel=
9&EntityId=Ar00900&AppName=1

The then DGP K. Chakravarty, who Bhatt said in his affidavit had made him attend and assist in the meeting, had refused to speak to the media about the 2002 riots investigation and no leads were coming forth from him.

Raigar was one of the key figures in both the Mumbai riots and the fake encounters that ensued, two unfortunate, and yet glaring examples of criminal conspiracy in Gujarat. V.L.Solanki, one of the police officers during the Sohrabuddin encounter investigation, had given a written statement to the CBI which was later included in the chargesheet. The statement said:

> In the first week of November, 2006, she (Ms Geeta Johri, IG) directed me to meet her in her chamber. Accordingly, I went to Gandhinagar. Initially, she had discussed the progress of the enquiry with me. After a little while, Ms Geeta Johri had told me that a horrible incident had occurred that day, that the MOS (Home) Shri Amit Shah had called her along with Additional DGP Shri G.C. Raigar and DGP Shri P.C. Pande at his office and had discussed about the progress of the inquiry.
>
> She had told me that the MOS (Home) was in a very bad mood, and that he had enquired from her about me, that how could a police inspector like me dare to write reports which could land senior officers like Shri D.G. Vanzara, Rajkumar Pandyan, who were responsible for the encounter of Sohrabuddin, into serious trouble.

Elaborating on the meeting, the SC had told the CBI that in the meeting Amit Shah held in December 2006 with the then DGP of Gujarat, PC Pande, ADGP, CID GC Raigar and IGP, CID Geeta Johri — then the lead investigator into the case — he had allegedly demanded that incriminating investigative reports prepared by Johri's deputy, Solanki, be altered. Solanki refused to cooperate. Instead, he sought to interview Prajapati, who was a witness to Sohrabuddin and Kausar Bi's abduction. Prajapati had shouted in open court in November 2006 that the police were going to kill him because he knew too much. A few days before he was to speak to Solanki, he too was 'encountered'.

After an investigation of over 18 months, CBI, in the chargesheet filed later had named Shah and 19 other accused, which included top cops Pande, Johri, O. P. Mathur, Rajkumar Pandian, D. Vanzara and R. K. Patel. They were accused of conspiring to eliminate Prajapati, a witness to the killing of gangster Sohrabuddin Shaikh in a fake encounter. Nine Gujarat Cadre IPS officers figured as witnesses: G.C.Raigar(then ADGP, CID Crime), Rajneesh Rai, I. M. Desai (then in CID crime and supervising the case), P. P. Pandey (ADGP, CID crime), V V Rabari (former head of CID crime), Rajan Priyadarshi (retd), Sudhir Sinha (then heading state IB), A. K. Sharma (DIG Crime Branch Ahmedabad) and Mayur Chavda (DySP, Chief Minister's Security).

CBI officers said Raigar and Rai were prime witnesses.

The chargesheet said that in mid-December 2006, Amit Shah (then MoS Home) called a meeting in his office—

attended by Pande, Johri and Raigar—to express his displeasure over the investigation of the Sheikh case. Shah asked Johri to destroy certain documents.

'While Raigar requested that he be kept out, Pande and Johri were willing collusive members of these conspiratorial instructions,' CBI said.

Raigar told the CBI that when the Sohrabuddin fake encounter case was handled by him, he was under constant pressure from the then junior home minister Amit Shah. 'He was unhappy with the work I was doing. He wanted to get some illegal work done through me, but this put me under a lot of stress. So, I sought a transfer. The same day, the home minister ordered for my transfer to Karai.' Another officer, O. P. Mathur, was given charge in his place. 'I told Shah to give me some days to carry out the transfer, but he transferred me the same day,' Raigar said.

He also said that the then PI V. L. Solanki, who was investigating the case, had never asked his permission to visit Udaipur regarding the case. The then ADGP O. P. Mathur in his statement said DySP G. B. Padheria and IGP Geeta Johri had had a disagreement after Johri had doubts that Padheria was responsible for turning a witness, Nathubha Jadeja, hostile. The entire episode was brought to the notice of the Principal Secretary (Home), who said they should sort it out themselves. This was later sorted out. However, Johri did not take him into confidence, he told the CBI.

The details of these statements emerged after I had left Gujarat in March 2011 after my sting operation.

In December when I first met Raigar in his office with Mike, he was still being summoned by the CBI to interrogate him. I explained the sensitivity of the situation to Mike and that there was a chance that we would not be able to elicit anything from him. 'Let's not ask him anything about politics today Mike, let's pretend like firangs we are absolutely out of the loop.'

Raigar took very well to Mike, asking him about his experience in Gujarat. Mike briefed him about his shoots at Amdavad ni gufa, Paldi and Sarkhej roza. I was not sure if it was just Gujaratis who were fascinated with anything foreign or American, or was it the conviction that both of us displayed that had these officers buying our story so readily.

I remember my conversation with Rahul Dholakia, a Gujarati and a filmmaker from Bollywood whose film *Parzania* based on the Gujarat riots was banned from screening in cinema houses in the state. Sitting at the Costa Coffee in Juhu, Mumbai, Rahul had me in splits when he regaled me with stories about his experience of getting funds and filming *Parzania*. His producer till such time that the Hindu right wing protested against the film had no idea that the film was against the injustice meted out to the minorities in the state during the riots. Rahul had worked for an American channel and he played the card of making a film on Gujarat for the NRIs. My narrative to most of those I met in Gujarat was similar. That was enough context for the producers and concerned authorities to repose faith in Dholakia. On one occasion when he wanted footage of Gujarat riots for the film, he approached a newspaper which had the relevant tapes. The man at the helm of affairs was impressed that he was from America. And even more impressed when he discovered that Dholakia's grandfather was the Chairperson of the Hindu Mahasabha. He was given immediate access to everything he needed.

The predicament at hand, however, was Raigar. In the first meeting with us he was more than willing to talk, giving me a fatherly lecture on not delaying my marriage further as after an age a girl finds it difficult to get a prospective match. He belonged to an old-fashioned family from Rajasthan and was finding it difficult to be a witness in the case against Amit Shah fearing his wrath. But with evidence against Shah mounting each day on his culpability in the fake encounters, Raigar had finally decided to be a witness. But what Raigar revealed on the second day of my conversation with him was stunning.

I knew the cast of characters in the fake encounters but the manner in which each of the characters had been manipulated and utilized by the dispensation was difficult to comprehend. Raigar was at ease because he knew that I had already spoken to P.C. Pande, Ashok Narayan, Rajan Priyadarshi and he was convinced that I was covering the glorious police force of Gujarat.

I spoke to him about the Bhuj earthquake and he gave us notes on the intensity of the quake and the number of lives that were lost, the strenuous work that the Gujarat police had had to undertake in the aftermath. With a great show of naivete I asked him if Gujarat was indeed as polarized as it was made out to be. 'Ah', he said, 'you have no idea what happened here in 2002.' My show of naivete turned into open curiosity as he spoke about the riots. I told him that I had some notes on it from the other officers. Raigar was the head of intelligence which meant he held a crucial post during the Gujarat riots.

Q) But tell me that Modi part,that everybody holds him responsible?

A) Don't make me talk about it? I have just gotten out of it.

Q You were in the midst of it when it was happening?

A) I was.

Q) Quite a sore point?

A) Yes, I want to forget those three months of the riots. Certain things happened which should not have happened.

Q) Really? Hurt your conscience too?

A) Yes, it did, it did.

Q) Ashok Narayan also said that.

A) Yes, he was also in the thick of things. It's still fresh in people's minds, it's everywhere. America still does not allow him [Modi]. In spite of being so popular. Recently in Wikileaks, it was said that America now wants to have good relations with him. But later the same Wikileaks said unceremonious things about him. So he came out in the media about the good part.

Q) But were these the worst [riots] that the country had seen. Worse than Mumbai?

A)   Yes, Mumbai was just for two days. This one lasted for months at a stretch.

Q)   But how? Why was it allowed to stretch for such a long time?

A)   That Narayan must have told you, he was the Home Secretary then.

Q)   Yeah, he said he was very upset. He was very critical of the government, that the state government didn't act.

A)   He was the Home Secretary. He was the most important functionary for the government. And what he's saying has to be the truth.

Q)   But were all of you disillusioned?

A)   Yes, most of us were disillusioned, pained, except those who were toeing the government line then, [they] sided with the government. It's not just politicians who were playing, even policemen were responsible.

Q)   So, was it more like a politician-police nexus during the riots?

A)   Limitedly yes, because once the situation goes out of hand, not much can be done.

Q)   But he [Modi] drew a lot of political benefit from that. He is what he is today because of the riots.

A)   Oh yes, absolutely. The very next election they were jittery. But this came in handy. They thought they had done this for him.

Soon after the conversation moved on to the fake encounters. Raigar was the additional DGP when the investigations were carried on. He had been grilled over 10-hour sessions each day in May and June of that year by the CBI about the fake encounters. Yet, he was happy to give his side of the story to me.

Q) What's with the encounters here? You were there.

A) I was in just one. One criminal [Sohrabuddin] was killed in a false encounter. What was foolishly done was they killed his wife.

Q) Some minister was also involved?

A) Home minister Amit Shah.

Q) It must have been difficult serving under him.

A) We disagreed with him. We refused to take his orders which is why we were saved from being arrested in the encounters.

Q) Is it as bad everywhere?

A) Gujarat was much better 10 years ago.

Q) Is it because of the political change?

A) In a democracy if a person becomes too big, it can be detrimental, like this minister, the home minister [Amit Shah]. He controls transfers, postings, promotions. And [if] somebody does not do his job, he's sent to a side posting and nobody wants to be sent to a side posting. Which is why I asked to be transferred during the Sohrabuddin case.

Q) Transferred because they didn't want you to investigate?

A) Because I didn't want to investigate in the wrong way.

Q) And they wanted YOU to investigate the wrong way?

A)   Yes.

Q)   How does a man get to do all this? How could Amit Shah be allowed to get away?

A)   He found his way. He was close to people in power.

Q)   He was close to the CM?

A)   Yes, he was very close to the CM. He was the closest to the CM.

Q)   So the CM could not protect him from being arrested?

A)   He could not do it [there was evidence against him]

Q)   Yes and then he would have himself got involved in it?

A)   If he interferes he goes, that way this fellow [CM] is clever. He knew everything but he kept a distance so he was not caught in it.

There is a law, you can't go on doing encounters. Even if you do because of one reason, you can't go about eliminating people. And for these ministers it's very easy, they go scot free, they don't have to sign, they do things verbally. But now with technology it's become very easy, they use phones which can be tracked.

Q)   Yes, in your case I was reading they got the minister in because of some call records?

A)   Yes.

Q)   But are there upright officers in the state unlike what we are seeing?

A)   Yes, there are a lot of them, but to do some damage

you just need some bad fish. However there are some good officers left because of which now ministers are being booked.

Q) Yes, somebody asked me to meet an officer called Rahul Sharma. He apparently is upright and so not in the good books of the government?

A) He's under scrutiny [by the government] for saving Muslim lives. He saved Muslim children in a school. Not only saved but he also arrested some people and [he] arresting a ruling party member so they got him transferred from his posting.

A) There was a problem from the government side, and initially they never realized the situation would be so bad. Initially they didn't want to use force against the rioters. Which is why things went out of control.

Q) Is it true that they wanted to go soft on Hindus [who were] against Muslims.

A) Initially yes, not realizing that it will get so bad. But what you said is true.

Q) But you officers were asked to go soft on Hindus, on rioters?

A) Not we, not in general, but people who mattered, in important positions in certain places, in certain areas they were communicated.

Q) Their was a CM called Keshubhai before Mr Modi? How was he?

A) In comparison to Modi, he was a saint. By comparison. I mean Keshubhai will not deliberately want somebody to be harmed. Whatever religion. He will not let them be harmed because they were Muslims.

Q) But sir, from a neutral point of view, for instance, a lot of facts seem to be mixed with fiction?

A) You know it's difficult. Because these people do not give direct orders, they are all invisible. In law also, look at it. For instance if the Chief Secretary says that I won't follow you and the CM says you have to, then whatever happens it is the responsibility of the CM. In the police force, however, it is my responsibility.

Q) Mr Chakravarthy made the same point. He said that certain orders were given but they were not given directly? And that's something that needs to be understood?

A) Yes, it's like they would tell it to people they had obliged in the past. They know who would help them. Informally they would talk to the inspectors and lower rung police officers. But not all officers would take their orders. There are certain officers at the top who still have convictions left.

Q) So it boomerangs if the CM tells them?

A) Yes, like the man you met in Gandhinagar, Ashok Narayan. He would not take anything. He would not say 'Yes sir'.

Q) Also he's an IAS Officer?

A) Yes, they receive orders on paper. Unlike us.

Q) Sir, also you brought up something interesting. For

instance, when you said that during the encounters investigation you were under political pressure; can't you then arrest the same people who pressurized you? For instance, this Home Minister?

A) There has to be certain evidence, This is the evidence available against us. I told that Shah that I won't do certain things when he asked me to. There are many who would say 'yes sir we would do it', because they had other interests.

Q) So the state can't really harm you if you directly went against the HM.

A) Well, not directly, unless they indirectly get me killed. But yes there is democracy here. So we can survive.

Q) I was reading up on you and apparently there is an allegation against your Home Minister Shah that he used to ask the officers concerned for witnesses, statements?

A) But he never got them. He indirectly would ask: who are the people who are speaking against me?

Q) What happened of Mrs Johri? She said that Sohrabuddin was a terrorist.

A) See, the point is not as much about Sohrabuddin as about his wife. Even if Sohrabuddin was killed in a right or lawful encounter it would not have been a problem. The point was the wife, why was she killed? And that too three days later.

Q) So you were investigating it?

A) We investigated when this entire thing about the

encounters being false came up. So Geeta did it, she was working under me. Till I was there she did a good job after that you know.... [smiles].

Q) Which is why you were transferred?

A) Yes.

Q) In fact, I also met P.C. Pande.

A) Oh, he was the Commissioner of Police.

Q) So you both were working together during the riots?

A) Yes, we had to, I was the IB Chief.

Q) And many officers whom I met said that the CM confided in Pande and got all the job done in the riots through him.

A) You know everything by now, about the riots [smiles]

Raigar had said everything. Indeed, he had left nothing unsaid. In every word he had said to us, the involvement of Modi, Shah and the complicit cops stared us in the face. I was simmering inside. Mike could feel my anger, he held my hand when we left Raigar's residence. It was brazen. Raigar had confirmed all the off-hand conversations on state complicity in the Gujarat riots and fake encounters.

Did Raigar not conclude that IPS officer Rahul Sharma was being victimized by the state for having saved the lives of Muslim students in a madrassa in Gujarat? Could we still believe that there was a media witchunt against the then Gujarat CM and his ministers? The evidence on these tapes stated otherwise.

My head was hurting. I longed for my family, I longed

for the warmth of my own people. I yearned to run away from the hatred that was being peddled in this unfortunate state, that was revealed to me each day by someone or the other. I needed a break.

I knocked on Paani's door. She had purchased some decorative handicrafts from a local artisan and was trying to fix them on her wall. When she opened the door, she said, 'Hey, help me' giving me a warm smile and went on talking about how beautiful Gujarat was. Yes, I mumbled. Yes indeed, if only Paani could see the hatred that I had seen. She was all of 18 like many of Gujarat's young population. Why were they being fed so much hatred? I didn't want to work for some time. I called up Ajay.

There was a college festival for which he had some passes. He offered to pick me up. I put on a black kurta, lined my eyes with kohl and wore make-up and heels. Mike who was reading a book close by refused to accompany me suggesting I become a college student for a day and go out dancing and have a good evening. I desperately needed it. That evening I felt that there was somebody parked outside the Nehru Foundation whom I had spotted there in the morning as well.

Perhaps it was just a hunch. Instead of taking an auto to the college where the festival was to take place, I messaged Ajay to pick me up. That evening I took pictures, danced with the students, sang out loud. The next day the car that had been parked outside the previous day was missing.

CHAPTER 8

P.C. Pande

Many in the force called him an ostrich while some described him as a most chivalrous, well-behaved officer who was articulate and suave. A man whom the CM trusted most and who had Modi's ear and Shah's on all pertinent matters in the state. He was a man whom loved the good things in life—foreign vacations, glowing reviews about himself, and evenings at the club or the gymkhana over drinks with friends.

The *Telegraph* newspaper dated 2 March 2002 wrote the following description about him.

> Former Commissioner of Police, Ahmedabad, Shri P.C. Pande (he was CP when the carnage took place). Nothing illustrates police role better than police commissioner P.C. Pande's statement that, 'Police were not insulated from the general social milieu… (When) there's a change in the perception of society, the police are part of it and there's bound to be some contagion effect.

I had made Mike call Pande and then followed it up by calling him myself to check the schedule. I could hear that he was impressed. When we entered his bungalow in Ahmedabad, he was was taking his wheelchair-bound mother for a round in the garden. 'Namaste,' I said to him and his mother. Mike was introduced as the assistant and we were ushered inside. The wife who we were told was undergoing treatment for cancer entered the living room to introduce herself. There were piles of newspapers and magazines, a copy of *India Today* and other Gujarati newspapers lying on the coffee table.

The first thing he asked me was about my second name Tyagi. I told him about my RSS roots, about my father, a Sanskrit teacher and my American credentials. That I was a Kayastha who had family in Mumbai and Kanpur and was far removed from religion. But I reassured him that the atmosphere of appeasement of Muslims in the country was bringing me closer to my religion.

It had the desired effect, but Pande was a shrewd man. He was curious if anybody had told us about his alleged dubious image in the media before meeting him. He was playing his cards well. I had not worn any of my equipment that day. I exclaimed that I had heard only good things about him from filmmaker Naresh Kanodia who was our only point of reference in Gujarat.

'Oh, now I get it,' he exclaimed, 'else you would have also come up with a prejudiced mind like the *Al Jazeera* and other yellow journalists of this country.' I told him I wanted to meet diamond traders from Surat who were well known across the world. I had done my homework. Pande's son ran a diamond business in Surat and he eagerly gave me his contact details. I also asked Pande to help me with somebody who was handling the films division or publicity division of Vibrant Gujarat about which we had heard such terrific things. 'I need to know about Kutch sir, the white sand, and the new highway and the state of the art technology that makes Gujarat stand out as one of the most vibrant states of India. Also something about its culture.'

Despite Pande's provocation about his controversial image during the riots, I reacted as if it held no interest for me. I was given the number of a gentleman called Thirupugzah, a South Indian bureaucrat who would give us all the relevant material on Gujarat, especially the Vibrant Gujarat campaign.

'And Maithili,' he exclaimed, 'you must also read this column by one of the most venerable intellectuals called Suhel Seth in a newspaper.' He had prepared himself well. There were ready printouts of all articles that lauded Modi along with a copy of an *India Today* issue which had Maulana Vastanvi of Deoband praising Modi, a statement which he said later was misquoted. Pande had at least 12 copies of the Suhel Seth column, one of which he handed over to me. Pande added, 'And if the film is for the Gujaratis in America, I am sure Modiji will be happy to speak to you. Let me know and I will fix the meeting.'

I showed little enthusiasm and said I would meet anyone Pande wanted me to because he came across as one of the most well-versed men in Gujarat and I would need his guidance on how to make the film. Pande seemed pleased with this.

We were not dealing with footsoldiers, I told Mike as we were eating our 20-rupee lunch at the canteen later. I handed over the fried papad in my plate to Mike who relished it. I told him that my colleague at *Tehelka* had in the past done a sting operation in Gujarat. But with thugs and rioters. Here we were dealing with seasoned diplomats, one needed to be extremely confident and convinced of the premise one had set. Mike suggested we write a film script once we were done with the sting. We laughed.

While meeting P.C.Pande, we also continued our sessions with Raigar, Ashok Narayan, Maya Kodnani, and all of them were told about our meetings with the others. I had a narrow escape one day when I was on my way to P.C. Pande's bungalow for a meeting. Just as I was approaching his house, I spotted an orderly of an official who knew me as Rana Ayyub stepping out of a bungalow just three houses away. Luckily my curly hair which is usually a dead giveaway was neatly tied and my bandana covered almost half my face. Pande was at the gate to receive me. Beads of sweat emerged at my hairline and trickled down my cheek. My body temperature had gone up. Pande noticed that I was sweating and the colour of my face had changed. 'Are you ok Maithili?' he asked, escorting me into his bungalow. Yes sir, I replied yet to recover from the fact that my cover might almost have been busted a minute ago. I mumbled that the change in weather might have given me a fever.

He immediately made me sit down, got his help to make

me a cup of coffee and went inside his room to get the
medical kit. He took out his thermometer and asked me
to place it below my tongue. I was shaking. He suggested
I accompany him to the doctor, I resisted saying it was
normal. The thermometer beeped at 99. He forced me to
eat a biscuit followed by a coffee and a paracetamol. I was
feeling better. I smiled and enquired about Mrs Pande who
arrived minutes later.

He was planning a trip to Nepal with his relatives or
so a telephone conversation with his brother indicated. I
calculated in my head that it meant little time for me to
get my act in place. He was planning to visit Kathmandu
during his year-end break and suggested some hip places
for me in the country to go visit on new year's eve. I nodded
in acknowledgement. During one of our conversations
while discussing Hindu-Muslim polarization in Gujarat,
Pande told me that one of his lawyers and friends who
dropped in frequently at his place was a Muslim. From
that day on every time I sat at Pande's residence I would
have palpitations as I was acquainted with this lawyer
from Ahmedabad whom I had met in relation to various
criminal cases he was dealing with. As my nerves played
havoc, the conversations with P.C.Pande flowed smoothly
in the months that followed.

Q) How integral is Gujarat to the RSS?

A)   You see, it is the backbone of the BJP of the Gujarat
     government. It is the only organization that could
     counter the Islamic parties.

Q)   And how close is he to the RSS?

A) Oh yes, he's very very close to the RSS. It's very key to him. He was a cadre.
The RSS chief here Amrutbhai Kadiwala wields a lot of power over him.

Q) I hear a lot rumblings about your ministers here whether it concerns riots or the state of affairs. The RSS here was very fond of Haren Pandya?

A) Yes, he was a very popular leader here, the Home Minister, Haren Pandya, he was very close to the RSS. For that matter we had Amit Shah here who is now behind bars. He was very close to the RSS. Another leader called Gordhan Zadaphia here, he was very close to the VHP in between.

Q) And all were Home Ministers. Is it a conscious decision to have them...?

A) Yes, because the Home Department controls the police officers so it's good to have your [own] men. So when Keshubhai was the CM, Haren Pandya was the HM.

Q) I should not meet Gordhan Zadaphia, you suggest?

A) No, I don't think you should meet him, because then you will deviate...I mean it's not a part of your film.

Q) Achcha, so if I am in Delhi, you are suggesting I meet Amit Shah?

A) Yes, you should, he's an ideologue.

Q) Why do you suggest I meet him?

A) You will get a different perspective of the state. He's very focused. He will tell you about the RSS and the state.

Q) Can I give him your reference? Where does he stay?

A) Yes, tell him that I asked. He stays at Gujarat Bhavan.

Q) Should I speak to Modiji about the riots?

A) Don't, he won't talk.

Q) It's like his Achilles heel?

A) Yes, do not.

Q) So, you were there during the riots?

A) Yes, it was one of the most horrific times of my life. I had already seen 30 years of service. But look at this; there were riots in 85, 87, 89, 92 and most of the times the Hindus got a beating. And the Muslims got an upperhand. So this time in 2002, it had to happen, it was the retaliation of Hindus. Also post-1995, people felt that the government was theirs, especially because it was a BJP government. They say I did not reach people. Not a single person called me, I am not a clairvoyant to figure who is calling me.

Q) So, Modi is the poster boy?

A) You know Mallika Sarabhai, that dancer, she is a big Modi basher. They say the riots of 2002 are because of him. He says I didn't go and burn the train at Godhra. So if I didn't do that, how can you blame me for whatever took place after that. If that had been done by me, this was also done by me. See, this was a reaction to what happened there. I mean if you see it logically, here is a group of

Muslims going and setting fire on a train, so what will be your reaction?

Q) You hit them back?

A) Yes, Yes, you hit them back, now this hitting back, you must have already done research that they [the Hindus] got a beating in 85, 86, 92 and so on, what happens, here is the chance, give it back to them.... Why should anybody mind it?

Q) And I am sure he would not have stopped it.

A) See once people get this passionate about it, you can't stop them, like in Egypt.

So you tell me would you want to open fire on a population like this?

What if he does? Will that fellow be allowed to walk the streets again? Now this kind of scenario, how do you say Modi should have put off the switch? The remote was not in his hands.

Q) How long did the riots last?

A) Then initial phase lasted for about 2 days and not more than that.

Q) So, Hindus were targeting Muslims was what the media projected ?

A) Yes, what else would they show? Muslims were targeting the Hindus also. You see correspondingly, ok, if not in as much percentage but here we are not matching evenness. Or [making it] evenly balanced. But then Muslims were the aggressors in the first place with the train burning at Godhra, so naturally the reaction would be there.

Muslims receive larger damage. But they also give back. So If a Hindu comes in the way he also gets killed. So this you ask him. He will speak out.

Q) By the way, I saw a write-up in the newspaper the day before on the SIT report?

A) Oh yes, there was an SIT committee that was formed to look into the riots so that was for that. The report was submitted in the Supreme Court and a copy of that was leaked to the media, this newspaper. Otherwise it was confidential. Otherwise the report does not blame him for anything.

But the person who has written the report says that he didn't find anything to pin him down.

Q) And didn't they try to pin you down too?

A) Oh yes, they said officers who worked for him were given postings post-retirement. I say what posting? Mine is a posting which does not give me any money.

Q) But again if you are working for the state why shouldn't he award you? Then should it be given to people who went against him?

A) Yes, why should he give postings to people who went against him?

Q) Of course not.

A) No question, no question.

Q) He's not a saint

A) That's what.

Q) You go on the road. Ask people, go across to Parimal Garden?

A) Yes, they love him.

Q), I guess also because he gave them what they wanted. He epitomizes what they want. Most of the people said that there was no minority appeasement and [they got] their gaurav back.

A) Yes, this is the feedback which is unsolicited.

Q) So, Muslims hate him

A) Those who are hardboiled, but they are seeing what they are seeing in the media, like you see that Deoband chief, Vastanvi. It's there in *India Today*, Vastanvi says that Gujarat gives equal opportunities. So this was objected to, because they thought he is giving Modi a certificate for what he did in 2002.
I was sitting at [Mukul] Sinha's place and I met some *Al Jazeera* channel reporters sitting there?

A) Oh yes, so the Muslim channel people would have come to cover the Godhra verdict. So they will talk some shit.

Q) So he basically gave me a copy of some periodical that comes out which had carried a report on the SIT.

A) Achcha, it must have been that *Communalism Combat*.

Q) No, No, let me tell you...it was *Tehelka*.

A) Oh, that's a classic example of yellow journalism. You know what the *Tehelka* people do, they go about carrying cameras so they shoot you. They will show one person giving money to the other, they will enact it and then they will say. Now you don't hear the conversation and this will be shown.

Q) How do they show it?

A) They sell it to channels. Earlier they showed some minister exchanging money with an arms dealer. So bits and pieces will be there but not the entire footage. For 2002, some of these extra garrulous people, they would show them. This is how they earn money. They will sell the footage to news channels. Like that Sinha, why does he have to give interview to *Al Jazeera*. That channel kept on showing how women were being raped and burnt. And why? Because it gives more mileage.

Q) You must have been grilled by the commissions?

A) Yes, I still am.

Q) So it's not coming to an end? You must have been questioned?

A) Yes, I have been questioned. It's going on, because with this stick, you can beat Narendra Modi.
For them 2002 is a full-time occupation, it reaps the money.

Q) I really wanted to know, I mean you were there as the Police Commissioner, so how did you deal with it?

A) It was terrible. I mean not that I had not seen a situation like this earlier but this was different. And like what happened in Egypt. You know now you can't use force on people in Egypt right so how does one use force on a crowd like that which was out protesting here. Would he have been able to exist after that? Force is not the answer.

Q) So did that Godhra lead to Gujarat?

A) Yes, a train was coming from Ayodhya, it had supporters of VHP, basically VHP people, they wanted a temple at Ayodhya. They were returning and there were 73 people, but some Muslims attacked them, locals came with petrol cans, entered the compartment and set it on fire. As a result 61 people died.

In retaliation VHP gave a call for bandh

Then [on the] 28th violence erupted and everybody was out on the roads. Old, young people, girls....

Q) So what's the accusation against him?

A) Their view is that he organized everybody to come out. 27th, he goes to Godhra....

A) That he orchestrated the violence against Muslims?

Q) Also the accusation is that he went to Godhra and did not even bother to visit the riot victims?

A) Why would he do that, meet them?

Q) Yeah, the Hindus were being killed?

A) And he came back at 10 or 11 pm

Q) There view is that he asked them to not act.

A) Yes, so they asked me that during the commission and I said I was given no such instruction. I said I had not received any such instruction from him. And I did, and in spite of that people get killed. Now I cannot say that I can protect everybody.

I am not god and as I said I tried to do my best.

Q) So is this the only thing?

A) No, they have only this thing against me. Because

this is the only way they can reach Narendra Modi, and that is through me.

Q) And also because you are very close to him?

A) Supposing I say anything against him, then they would be happy.

Q) So, you must have made a lot of enemies, including in the force?

A) There could be a couple of IPS officers.

Q) Like I was told about the handful of ones who were doing a good job here?

A) Yes Rahul Sharma, Satish Verma, Kuldeep Sharma, they are the ones.

Q) Yes, Yes.

A) That Kuldeep Sharma. He's been sent to the Sheep and Wool [department]. He's on the wrong side of the government now and right side of people like Mukul Sinha.
    You see it's a long story, you have to know the entire thing. Kuldeep Sharma picked up cudgels with the then Home Minister.

Q) And who was that?

A) Amit Shah.

Q) The same person who was arrested?

A) Kuldeep Sharma complained to the CM that your HM is a scoundrel, so the CM must have asked him to prove [it].

Q) But how will he act against the HM?

A) And listen then he has the cheek to write a letter to the CM so as to get a CBI inquiry into that matter, against the HM. But the CM said I will get this enquired by a retired Chief Secretary.

Q) So he must have been happy when Shah was arrested?

A) He was instrumental in getting him arrested.

Q) But how?

A) He was the one who gave the evidence to the CBI as well as to the media. So he proved the call records of an officer called Pandian.

Q) How?

A) Pandian and Kuldeep had some other cases against each other. Pandian exposed one case in the newspaper. So he [Kuldeep] wanted to send Pandian to jail. And Pandian was indeed involved in the encounter.

Q) Oh, that's how he got the HM.

A) Yes, because Pandian was close to the HM. He would speak to him. Therefore he proved that Shah was involved in the encounter.

Q) So, who are the people whose encounters were done?

A) All of them are scoundrels and petty criminals and when the law can't do much you eliminate them.

Q) I even heard some woman, lady was also encountered calling her a terrorist.

A) Yes, Yes.

So what I was saying is, that I was the DG and I was retiring from the force and by that time he also came from abroad. So he wanted to be the DG of

Police. But the point was how do you appoint him, a man who would always be upto some mischief against the government?

Q) Yes and he had gone against the government so how could they?

A) Yes, you don't expect them to appoint a man like him [Kuldeep Sharma], so he was given a side posting.

Q) Like what?

A) He was made the Chairman of the Sheep and Wool department. [laughs]

Q) Oh ****, that's like a punishment posting!

A) It was, it was meant to be a punishment posting. If you go against the government then I mean.... I mean otherwise he was the most qualified person to be the DG.

He also did a Phd in policing and reforms. But he just wanted to take revenge so from there it began.

The CM always said that he was very unreliable. In fact he was very good with the HM.

Q) But the HM is quite a character?

A) But I would advise you to meet him, he's on bail but the condition is he can't go to Gujarat. So I would advise you to meet him. He's a brilliant guy. Very sharp. Lot of interesting things.

Q) A man of ideology?

A) Yes, he is core RSS.

Q) Why is all this happening?

A) But the likes of Teestas and Sinhas will like this. See, whatever you say, the 80 per cent janta is of the majority, the Hindus, so you have to look after them. Like the Congress does. And why do you have to pander to the illegal doings of the Muslims. Muslims however much they do wrong, you want to support them. Hindus however much they do right, you go against them?

Q) But the Hindus would have felt so liberated?

A) Yes yes, now go take a walk in the city and see in the city in the Hindu and Muslim dominated areas We had to sift through so many call records .That's how the IM guys were caught [Gujarat blasts]

Q) Wow!

A) And the Supreme Court says don't conduct their cases.

Q) Why?

A) Minority appeasement.

Q) That happens in the SC too?

A) Yes, it does.

These people should be put against the wall and shot dead. You know one explosion takes place, 6 people die and then another and the third take place at the hospital near the trauma centre and that's where the patients come. So I rang the CM and said don't go. He had reached the Commissioner's office by then. The bomb was kept in a van.

You see the deviousness of these things. Now you want to appease them. What for? Votes.

My best friend is a Muslim but that's a different thing, that's just a person. Treat them like everybody, I have no problem.

Q) I am glad Muslims were taught a lesson during the riots.

A) Yes, you feel that, at one point of time ki jo hua theek hua, which is why I am so happy that I could get these people behind bars [Muslims]. It was the most satisfying thing.

So people like Mukul Sinha and Teesta will say there is anarchy. Yes there is anarchy but who created that anarchy, these very Muslims.

And not that I have any great love for political parties, but if the Congress is like this, I might as well be with the BJP.

Q) How do you feel about encounters?

A) See, personally I am against encounters, it's like a murder, but at times it becomes necessary.

Q) Yeah, so this officer that I spoke to, he was telling me about this encounter.

A) Achcha, that's when my name must have come up. I was the DG, but not during the encounter. The encounter took place in 2005. I was asked to investigate the case.

Q) Oh ok.

A) That person Sohrabuddin was being convicted on charges of [holding] some AK, there was the recovery and later [he was] convicted... that was his background. That female [Kausar Bi] was not even his wife.

Q) They had an affair?

A) She was living in with him. So if you stay in the company of a man of that nature, something that happens to him will also happen to you. Inviting trouble. And it's not that you are not aware of what this man is all about. Not that this is reason for any man to be killed.

Q) But Sir, did they do it for money or for ideology, for the Hindutva ideology?

A) Both, ideology as well as the money part.

Q) Which is what I have been told that corruption was a major reason for the encounter? Money was. Which is why both the HM and the officers were caught?

A) Oh yes, most of the time money goes into it.

Q) Many were saying that the CM was almost involved because of this HM.

A) See, the people who wanted the case to be investigated were people who were not the HM, the target was the CM.

Q) But the truth is that the HM indeed was involved hence....

A) See, technically by that benchmark you can't involve the CM.

Q) Give me some dope on this Singhal Guy, who heads the ATS. I am profiling him as a Dalit.

A) Singhal, otherwise good officer, he's from Rajasthan settled in Gujarat but he also was there in the Sohrabuddin encounter. They picked him also, he barely escaped and then he was in the Ishrat encounter.

Q) That's like a dent in the image of the government?

A) Yes, it is, kya kar sakte hain.

Q) All those officers who were there in 2002, did their image suffer a dent, even amongst Gujaratis?

A) Even Gujaratis felt that some officers could have done better. They did not stand up, they do not acquit themselves. I was treated as a neutral officer.

Q) But you are being persecuted?

A) No, but Gujaratis are not persecuting me, the NGOs are.

See, one, the bodies were brought in to Ahmedabad, and kept at the civil hospital. And after that there was some tension in the area. Information was trickling in that there were some cases coming in from here and there. My only regret is that I could not myself go to these two places where the violence had erupted because I am sure otherwise I could have not allowed it to happen at Naroda and Meghaninagar.

At one place then there is an ex-Parliamentarian who decides to take on 10,000 people from the rooftop of his society. Picks up his 12 bore gun and fires at the crowd.

Q) Who's this person?

A) Ehsaan Jaffrey, an old man around, 75 years old. He was formerly a member of the Rajya Sabha, now he opened fire. That firing resulted in two people dying and this is a part of police records. The aggression came from [the thought] what do I do. I am in strength of 10,000 you are in strength of 100, I won't do that.

Q) Why would I spare you then?

A) Exactly. You can say police ne kuch nahi kiya, now we didn't tell you to open fire, you could have kept quiet. This is the thing. Same thing happened at Naroda. There also one over-enthusiastic Hindu boy climbed on a mosque. Now Muslims, they chopped him into pieces. Hindus were agitated and that led to the riots.

Q) I was asked to meet a social activist called Teesta?

A) The biggest scoundrel ever. Take the number of this guy Uday Mahurkar, he's a journalist with *India Today*.

Q) And another lawyer called Sinha?

A) Another scoundrel.

He is fighting in the Nanavati Commission, and he gets money in loads from all these people abroad. And then there is this woman called Teesta Setalvad who belonged to the Setalvad family. And there is this guy called Javed Anand, who was a sub-editor then. At that time Javed was married. So she got to know them. Now her father did not like this. Javed disowned his earlier wife and moved in with her. And from there this Teesta had no standing but post-2002 she landed in Gujarat and promptly took up the cause of citizens in Gujarat. Because she was from a legal family, she got together retired judges and they also later came with a book called Communalism. And she started supporting the victims and money started coming in from the Middle East. And everybody thought that BJP will lose. But although the BJP won in Gujarat it lost power at the centre and hence she became the poster girl for the centre.

Q) Could you not do anything to stop her?

A) How could we? We wanted to but the courts would have pounced on us.

Q) So the CM would have confided in you [about] his worry [regarding her]?

A) Yes, he did.

Q) But see, Modi was made Modi by the riots right?

A) Yes, before that who knew him? Who was Modi? He came from Delhi, before that Himachal. He was in charge of the unimportant states, neither Haryana nor Himachal.

Q) This was like a trump card, no?

A) That's what…. if this had not happened, he would not have been known internationally. That gave such a push, although negative, at least he became known.

Q So, are you like his man?

A) I mean yes, considering I was there with him during the 2002 riots so it's OK.

These conversations have been recorded over a span of two months of meetings and conversations with various equipments. Pande who considers himself a favourite of Modi does not shy away from talking about his proximity to Modi. He has no qualms telling me that Modi is no saint to give postings to those who are ideologically opposed to him. He justifies the murder of Kausarbi saying that she was 'living in' with Sohrabuddin who was killed in a fake encounter as already proved by the CBI.

At various points in the conversation every time there is a reference to activists, he does not shy away from describing them as scoundrels who have brought Gujarat a bad name.

Towards the end I was not very astonished when he said that I should now go for a walk in Parimal Garden and see how Gujaratis feel liberated after the riots.

Pande offered to make me meet his son in Surat, who was a diamond trader, on his return from Nepal. He also helped fix a meeting with Amit Shah in Delhi who after getting bail in the fake encounters case was barred from entering Gujarat by the court. He also spoke to Thiru and asked him to help me with all the promotional narratives on Gujarat and the work done by the CM in getting investment in to the state. Pande was being probed by various commissions, and he was accused by the CBI in the fake encounters case. Ehsan Jaffery's wife had petitioned the Supreme Court for his inaction in saving her husband and other Muslims. But he was not bothered. As he told me nonchalantly he won't be touched.

By the time my conversations with Pande were coming to an end, my anxiety attacks had increased considerably. I wanted to leave the city for a while. This became possible when I planned to interview Chakravarty, the DG of Gujarat during the riots next as he was a resident of Mumbai. Chakravarty stayed in the cosmopolitan Khar area of Mumbai. Paani wanted to travel to Mumbai with me. And since Mike had to travel to Delhi again, and I needed an assistant, Paani and I took the next flight out to Mumbai. She carried with her a saree that was gifted to her by a colleague at office because one of my closest friends was getting married and I had invited Paani to the wedding celebrations. I promised Paani a glimpse of Indian culture once work was done.

CHAPTER 9

Chakravarthy

I had asked Ashok Narayan to put in a word of recommendation to Chakravarthy who was a bit of a recluse when it came to the media and his peers from the Gujarat officialdom. He had been hounded by the media, international press and commissions because he was the Director General of Police during the Gujarat riots. He lived a life of comparative tranquility with his wife and two daughters in the posh suburban area of Khar in Mumbai.

I had left Paani at home when I went to meet him. When my family members called me Nimmi as opposed to Maithili, Paani would be baffled. I told her that it was my nickname. But my mother found it very annoying every time Paani would refer to me as Maithili. One day when I was in the kitchen trying to fix breakfast for myself and Paani, she reacted, 'Why do you have to bring all the drama and acting you are doing in your office to your home. It's a house, not a theatre.' She was clearly miffed. It was not the change of name that bothered her, but the fact that I seemed to be living my life on the edge had begun to scare her. She feared for me. On one occasion I saw her crying in my room. She was holding one of my kurtas. 'It's very easy for them to bump you off, Sonu. I get nightmares that a truck has crushed you or that snake you stay with at that godforsaken house has bitten you.' I started laughing, hugged her, and assured her that nothing would ever happen to me. She kept sobbing.

I had taken an AC bus to Bandra from where I had to take an auto to Khar where Chakravarthy lived next to a well-known school. In the same building lived a doctor due to whom the building was famous among locals. I was ushered into the house by Chakravarthy himself who introduced me to his gorgeous wife who hailed from a royal family. The lighting of the living room was very dim and that had me worried. How would I be able to record any footage in the low lighting? And what excuse could I give them should I have to ask them to switch on the tubelights?

Chakravarthy asked me about my life in the United States and his wife informed me that her daughter was an aspiring actress living in the US. She encouraged me to get in touch with her actress daughter as both of us could be good friends, she thought. They had another daughter who came home as I was chatting with Mrs Chakravarthy. The younger daughter was a stewardess with a leading airline and chatted with me about how uncouth celebrities could be on flights. I met Chakravarthy three times over a period of one month. The first visit was very short and I restricted myself to sharing the details of my shooting in Kutch and meeting various potters there and attending the famous Uttarayan festival of Gujarat. I told Mrs Chakravarthy of the delicious tandoori paneer her friend and Ashok Narayan's wife had served me on one of the lunch invites. Mrs Chakravarthy soon became comfortable enough with me to show me her collection of sarees and family photographs.

I promised to visit them again the following week which I did. This time I carried a box of pedas for Mrs Chakravarthy who introduced me to a variety of snacks over coffee. But Chakravarthy was a man of few words. He had built a world for himself with few visitors and friends, mostly from his professional circle. His wife said that on the few visits they made to Ahmedabad, they felt out of place. Her husband, she said, was treated as an outsider despite being a man of integrity.

I knew exactly how to break his silence while speaking to his more-than-willing-to-talk-better-half. I dropped names of all the officers I had met in Gujarat and narrated all the gossip I had heard. All this as part of a superlative display of naivete and awe. It worked by breaking the ice.

Before I start to write about my conversations with Chakravarthy it is important to share some news items which appeared in Gujarat-based newspapers about him after the mainstream media accused him of being an inefficient DG who could not control the communal fire which had engulfed the state of Gujarat in 2002. He was in the news around the time I met him for refuting the report carried in various newspapers that Sanjiv Bhatt was present in the meeting called by Narendra Modi on 27 February 2002. However most of the witnesses who had corroborated Sanjiv Bhatt's version including a constable later said they had been coerced by him. Evidently, there was not much heft in Sanjiv Bhatt's claims. However, in the same year, SIT inquiry officer A.K. Malhotra confirmed the presence of eight men at the meeting: Chief Minister Modi, Acting Chief Secretary Swarna Kanta Verma, Additional Chief Secretary (Home) Ashok Narayan, DGP K. Chakravarthy, Ahmedabad Commissioner of Police P.C. Pande, Secretary (Home) K. Nityanandam, Principal Secretary to CM P.K. Mishra, and Secretary to CM Anil Mukim.

Chakravarthy was clearly one of the most critical names when it came to the investigation into the Gujarat riots and Gujarat under Narendra Modi and Amit Shah not just during the 2002 riots but during other critical periods of criminal investigations. On March 2002, *TOI* published a report that DGP Chakravarthy had fired a salvo at the Gujarat government over police transfers.[17]

On my second visit to the Chakravarthy residence he broke his silence at last on my spy camera. There were reports of him having taken a stand on behalf of his officers but none could have been substantiated. After all, he had refused to speak to the media as well as to his colleagues.

As I narrated various anecdotes from my meetings with

---

17 http://timesofindia.indiatimes.com/city/ahmedabad/Gujarat-DGP-fires-a-salvo-at-govt-over-police-transfers/articleshow/4994912.cms

other officials, Chakravarthy finally began to open up, perhaps because he realized that I already had access to too many off-the-record conversations. I finally had him speaking about the riots in Gujarat.

'It was the worst one could ever witness. The long and short of it is that there was no rational grounds to the riots. Here the riots followed the burning of the train at Godhra. Now no doubt the compartment belonged to the VHP guys who had gone into Ayodhya. The full train was theirs. So what had happened was [that] rioting followed. What [I] am saying is [that] normally when riots take place there is a cause and mostly local. Here was a cause that seemed to threaten the Hindu community at large.

'Now in riots who are the people who participate in riots. Poor people....Here all the rich people were on [the] streets. Some people called up to say, "Sir, Shoppers Stop mein Mercedes mein log aakar loot rahe hain."

'Since time immemorial History has taught Hindus that Ghazni and Babar invaded India and plundered Somnath. So this has been ingrained in the pschye of Hindus here. And riots have taken place in India since 1965. Thousands were killed earlier too.'

Q) What really went against him [Modi] I guess was the fact that he was from the RSS and he supported the RSS and the VHP during the riots?

A) That compulsion was inevitable. A person who has grown up as an RSS cadre, he has to bow down to their demands.

Q) That's what I was told that during the riots he bowed down to the RSS.

A) In his position he could not have done anything else, especially if you have been groomed by an organization which was involved. And this especially if you are a power hungry minister.

Q) Is he very power hungry?

A) Yes.

With due respect to Tehelka.

Q) What is that?

A) It's a magazine published by Tarun Tejpal, you must have heard of it.

It says that all officers during the riots were rewarded. Nothing personal but what did I get. It is alright, but it's wrong to tar everyone with the same brush, [it] is prejudice.

Q) Is it not because most of the people who were serving with you found themselves embroiled in controversies or had a role to play so you also came in the line of fire?

A) But then you can't do much about it.

Q) But the kind of person that you are it must have been difficult to survive as the DGP of Gujarat.

A) My approach was within my powers I would do my best. I tried to help as many Muslims as I could. A large number of people were saved; just because Ehsan Jaffrey was not saved....

Q) Who's Ehsaan Jaffrey?

A) He was a Muslim ex-MP who could not be saved.

He was killed by the mob. His house was burnt. The entire pocket was attacked. Police could not reach on time.

Q) Is it because you were the DG you got the flak?

A) See, under me too many people work...there is a hierarchy. Commissioner of Ahmedabad, his IG and then his junior. I gave orders to the Commisioner, I did ask him but the Commissioner says that he told his officers but by the time they went he [Ehsan Jaffrey] was already killed, the damage was done. So the Nanavati judicial enquiry is looking [at this] and the Supreme Court too has taken cognizance of this.

Q) That's what I am saying. You are paying for what others did and they are now reaping the rewards via the state?

A) That is inevitable.
Which is why I am saying that the media has been biased, it has not heard both sides of the story.

Q) You were never their favourite because of the stance you took during the riots?

A) I believe so. I never became that. Somehow I always felt like expressing whatever I did. It wasn't gibberish.

Q) You expressed your displeasure then during the riots?

A) Yes, certain points I brought to notice but then there are hierarchies and hierarchies which you have to face.

Q) You didn't have direct to access to CM?

A) See there is a system, you cannot dictate to the government. There is a course of action, there is a system. After a point you can't do much. You bring to the notice of the government certain things and if they do not take action what can you do beyond that?

Q) Were you upset that no cognizance was taken of whatever inputs you were giving?

A) Yes, but then this is a part of the game.[18]

Q) But you should write or speak about this? What really happened during the riots?

A) My daughters have been suggesting that....

Q) So what about the inquiries being set up to look into the riots?

A) One was the Banerjee Committee Report which said there was a conspiracy, but that had nothing to do with the judicial process so that can't be taken into account as there were no witnesses who were cross-examined. Then there is the Supreme Court-appointed SIT which is set to look into the individual cases. Then there is the Nanavati Commission set up by the state.

Q) You were grilled by all?

A) Yes.

---

18 This admission was important as Chakravarthy had pleaded amnesia over the role of the state in the Nanavati Commission and had given ambivalent statements on various occasions.

Q) Whose was more effective?

A) Well, the Nanavati [Commission] was more effective for them. You know what I am saying.[19]

Q) The government you mean?

A) Exactly. See, their people, [the] prosecution, Muslim defence lawyers. See, I am not going to the media to talk, I will talk before the proper commission.

Q) And the SC-appointed one should be neutral?

A) It so happened that Ehsaan Jaffery's wife, his widow, she was the one who complained.

Q) Your Home Minister was also arrested? Did you serve under him?

A) Oh yes, I had daggers drawn with him always.

Q) During the riots?

A) No, post riots, he came in after Akshardham.

Q) And you can't serve [under] a man who is corrupt?

A) Not just corruption, it's also the mindset. He got arrested. There were call records which were incriminating evidence.

Q) In what capacity were you serving under him?

A) DG.

Q) So you were saved?

A) Well, no, he gave me enough botheration.

Q) Did you feel claustrophobic during the riots? Did you fight?

---

19 When Chakravarthy says that the Nanavati Commission was more effective for the government he suggests that the commission which was formed under Justice Nanavati was favourable towards the Modi government.

A) Well, I have fought. Fight from within also requires a different kind of thing. One thing is to be a bravado [sic] or go to the public and press. In fact TOI wrote against me saying if Mr Chakravarthy had a conscience, he would have resigned. Why should I have resigned?

Was I the perpetrator? Was I the one conniving with the rioters? On the other hand I was trying my best to save the people. I was also apprehensive that the person who may succeed me might help them.[20]

Q) That could have happened had you not been around?

A) Yes.

Q) Had the bandh call not been given things would have helped?

A) Of course, it was given by the VHP.

Q) Which was like the centre.

A) Well VHP was an arm of the BJP, the ruling party.

Q) Did he give the orders not on act?

A) They didn't give any illegal orders to me. He won't sign his death warrant.

Q) Orders can be given invisibly?

A) It will be on a one-on-one basis, not in front of 20 people out of which 5 may be against you.[21]

---

20   Chakravarthy suggests here that he did not resign for fear of another officer joining as DG who would further connive with the government in systematically targeting the Muslim community during the riots.

21   The reference here is to the meeting on 27 February in which Modi

Q) So the book that you intend to write, will it ruffle feathers in the bureaucracy and the police force?

A) Well, as long as I don't name them and just share anecdotes.

Q) So, were you marginalized since the incidents?

A) Well, I had a friend in the form of Ashok Narayan whom I would agree with. Subbarao, the Chief Secretary also a friend, but not really, because I did not agree with what he did.

Q) What's with this Bhatt thing, that stuff that you were speaking of that day. The website you mentioned carried his testimony? Was it true?

A) It's not true in the sense that he was an SP-level officer. SP in the intelligence. And Mr Raigar was the Additional DG who was absent that crucial day. So he must have thought he should go and represent. But since it was a meeting of heads of departments, so he was not a participant. Mr Ashok Narayan will have to confirm what I am telling you.

---

allegedly asked his officers to go and kill Muslims. From various versions that I gathered during the sting operation, nothing suggests that Modi gave an order of this nature. However, what Chakravarty and Ashok Narayan both said was that orders were given to individual state officials. P.C.Pande almost corroborates it when he concludes that a Chief Minister could not be so naïve as to take such a risk in such a sensitive situation and during the first riots in the country's history to be covered live by the mainstream media.

Q) I met some of your friends by the way at Dafnala. All the officers, PC, PP....

A) Yes, they all stay there. Then there is Kuldeep Sharma.

Q) Oh yes, P.C.Pande was saying you should meet this man who is now in the Sheep and Wool Department.

A) Kuldeep is a nice guy, he's cut up with the government hence he has been kept aside. He had an attitude earlier that he was the defacto CM. Otherwise he's a good officer, he should have been the DG today but he has been kept aside only because he went against [them]. And what they do is so that they do not go to court, the government is so intelligent that he will give him a side posting. That Modi is a very intelligent man.[22]

Q) Achcha that Subbarao, nobody likes him? Narayan's wife, said he will tomtom the government.

A) The Chief Secretary. He has been rewarded by them so he's bound to talk only about the good stuff.

---

22 Chakravarthy is talking of Kuldeep Sharma who was in line to be the DG of Gujarat but the Gujarat government re-opened a 20-year-old case of an encounter in Bhuj against him. Allegedly because Sharma challenged Amit Shah, the Home Minister of Gujarat in a cooperative scams case. Shah was also livid with both Kuldeep and Pradeep Sharma because allegedly they were the whistleblowers in the Snoopgate scam in which Amit Shah was recorded instructing G.L.Singhal to snoop on a woman. He is also recorded saying that this had to be done on the instructions of 'Saheb' which is assumed to be a reference to Narendra Modi.

Q) So, Subbarao was the one hand in glove with the government during the riots?

A) Yeah, yeah, totally, very close to the boss.

Chakravarthy here makes reference to Subbarao, the Chief Secretary of Gujarat, whom everybody I met described as being the CM's man during the Gujarat riots.

A newspaper report described Subbarao as 'A former chief secretary who retired in 2003, he was rewarded with the chairmanship of the Gujarat Energy Regulatory Commission (GERC). This position is normally held by retired judges in Gujarat and analysts thought that they know why this reward came to him.'

Q) By the way your name was also there as the people who sided with the government?

A) Yeah, the magazine [*Tehelka*] said I had got benefits. What have I been rewarded [with]? All others have been rewarded, the Chief Secretary, the Home Secretary, the Police Commissioner.

    The point is, a person is trying to be objective then this should not happen.

Q) But even the Sanjiv Bhatt thing, he also named you?

A) Yeah, you should also meet Sreekumar. Are you talking about the minister coming to my office. That minister was there in my office for a short time, his name is I.K.Jadeja, he was very angry with me. He said, aapko fursat nahi hai mere saath baat karne ka. And I didn't want him to be in my room. So I told my chap to make him sit in the other room. I was busy with my controls, so this Sanjeev

guy must have seen him in the other room.
So there is no question of his interference.

Q) But even if Bhatt was there, nobody today will say that. Nobody will want to stick their neck out?

A) See, if that is the gospel truth, my limited answer to that is that the government appointed a judicial commission and this announcement was made in March in [the] Assembly. Now thereafter when the riots subsided and then these people who claimed they are the repository of all information, why didn't they do [anything]? Within a reasonable time they could have filed an affidavit. So this Sreekumar did it. He filed about five affidavits.

Q) But the tagline of this article in *Tehelka* says that this man can tell the truth?

A) I had asked him. Because Mr Raigar got transferred in the month of May. And then the riots were still going on. So this Sreekumar got posted as Additional DG intelligence. So I asked him to file an affidavit. So he did. Of his own accord, not a word about me and the others. And after a couple of months, he filed another one in which he said Mr Chakravarthy said this and that. So I gave a reply why did Mr Sreekumar not file an affidavit then. If he was such a Ramachandra ki aulad, he should have gone ahead and said this then. It is because he was bypassed for promotion. Now I had shifted to Mumbai.

This is not to be ever quoted. So this man used

to call me every day saying, Sir can you please come to Gujarat because I have to file a case in CAT against the government. Against his non-promotion. I said I cannot come because I am in Mumbai and several times they [his family] took the calls. So he said, Sir, all you have to say before CAT is whatever Sreekumar is saying is the truth. So I said how can I say something like this. And where is 2002 and 2005. Why talk of this today? So he wrote three affidavits against me, incriminating me. He sits at home making diaries, it's not an official case diary.

So this Bhatt is also his Jaatwaala.

And these very people when the going was good, they were with the government.

Q) So the meeting of Jadeja was the controversial meeting?

A) No, the meeting of CM.

Q) So the Bhatt chap was in this meeting?

A) No, as I said, Raigar was absent in this meeting so Bhatt by his own accord decided to be a part of the meeting.

But Ashok Narayan felt that since it was a meeting of the heads, he was not to be allowed. So if you want to fish in troubled waters, you can go and show your face.

Whereas in the case of Swarnakanta Verma, she had the legitimate locus standi to come.

Q) So everything or everybody is mired in the controversy, either encounters or riots.

A) Yes, yes, like a Home Minister has also been arrested.

Q) All the officers dislike him?

A) Yes, yes, everybody hates him.

Q) But why is a man like him, serving as Home Minister?

A) Because of the political connections. Amit Shah and I had daggers drawn [for each other]. Kuldeep registered a case against him when he was in ACB.

Q) So what did Shah do to you?

A) Well, on paper I never signed.

Q) Why didn't you all complain?

A) Politically he was too strong. As long as they were giving written orders. And the only good thing was that he would sign the letters himself, not even the PA. He would first try to reason ki inko badalna hai, inko change karna hai. But later he would himself sign orders. So he would sign orders that were to be done by junior functionaries, first time in the history of the country.

Q) What orders?

A) Transferring officials. Ye mera aadmi hai, usko yahan rakho. So I would tell him, Sir government orders dega to main karega, so promptly next day the orders would come. So Ashok Narayan was saved the agony of Shah.

Q) And then there was this minister Maya Kodnani?

A) Oh yeah, she was involved in the Naroda case. The matter is up in the SC.

Q) But she looked so innocent. Was she really involved?

A) She was, RSS walas, looks can be deceptive.

Chakravarty is a conflicted man who has bitter truths about his own men in uniform who according to him spoke much too late (like Sreekumar) for justice to be done. One may agree that Sreekumar spoke a bit too late and that Sanjiv Bhatt's version of the truth does not carry heft or present tangible evidence, but does that absolve Chakravarthy of all responsibility as DG of state? Indeed, it becomes extremely difficult for a DG or any other official in the police ranks to take on the high and the mighty in the government. In this case, they were dealing with Amit Shah, who all of them, including Singhal, Raigar, Ashok Narayan, Priyadarshi and now Chakravarthy concur was a man least concerned about law and order and gave illegal orders to officials. But was Chakravarthy by maintaining silence bringing the perpetrators of communal violence to justice?

CHAPTER 10

Maya Kodnani and the others

I had almost begun enjoying my life in Ahmedabad, or as Ajay would say, I seemed to be turning into a true Amdavadi. I knew how to manage an apple pie from Upper Crust (a famous bakery) in Ahmedabad at 1am. The girls from the hostel and I would go for an outing at 2am to eat eggs. Between the Durga Puja pandal and nine days of garba, Paani and I had danced our feet red.

We had discovered a lunch place which served the best Kathiavad ghatia and lunch menu dishes lovingly garnished with red chillies. On one of the occasions when I had to vacate the room at the Nehru Foundation for three days I found space at the NID hostel as a student. I shared the room with a student who would be up till the wee hours of the morning chatting with her boyfriend. Having wanted to stay in a hostel all through my student life I was truly enjoying this aspect of my time in Ahmedabad.

However, not everything was making me happy. It was

finally time for Mike to leave. We went to Pakwaan, his favourite thali joint, for his farewell dinner. His laptop had some stunning portraits of Ahmedabad, and by now he had learnt to speak reasonably good Hindi. We spoke all night before retiring to our respective rooms. He had a flight to Delhi at 10am. The next morning I found a picture and a peacock feather under my door. The picture was of Lord Krishna, and behind it Mike had scribbled in Hindi, Pyaari Maithili, apna khayal rakhna. My friend, my comfort, my partner in crime had left me. I had no one left to talk to who knew Rana Ayyub. Mike would come back to Ahmedabad for one day later in 2011 for the final act.

When I entered Ahmedabad again, it was some time in 2013 to get hold of some documents. Maya Kodnani was back behind bars. The sting was done and I was still waiting for it to see the light of day while continuing to work for *Tehelka*. The officer whom I was meeting for the documents told me that he had met Mayaben in jail. He said he was thinking of sending Osho books to Mayaben in jail. I was surprised at the statement. He said, 'She kept crying, asked me to take her out, she's bordering on insanity. I thought she could take help from spirituality.'

On one of my afternoon lunch visits during the sting to Mayaben's place, she had served me aamras. We were past the mango season but she had puréed the mango and stored it in the freezer for her son who was to visit her from the US soon. Then she hugged me and said 'You eat, it will feel like my son is eating. You too are like my daughter Maithili.'

I had that afternoon explained to her the Gita Saar which I had allegedly learnt from my Sanskrit teacher father. She was impressed that a girl who had lived abroad had more knowledge about religion that those who lived here. 'I say Maithili, we have lost all our culture. Look at these Muslims, even their kids are so kattar.' I nodded in agreement. The lunch was a simple fare of two vegetables, papad and pooris. Mayaben had cooked the meal herself and she served me as I ate.

That evening we began to talk. There was no doubt about the hatred she had for the Muslim community but more than anything else it was her disdain for Modi which emerged in her conversation with me. She minced no words in suggesting that Modi had conveniently used cases against her and Gordhan Zadaphia to eliminate the people he did not like.

'This new generation here, has got nothing, no ideology, even if anything happens, it will never come on the streets.

'See in our religion what they teach, do not even hurt an ant and from [the] beginning our child is taught this. And what are these people taught from childhood, that you have to kill, only if you kill, you are a Muslim. Ye log kya sikhaate hain ki aap ek aadmi ko bhi musalmaan baanao toh aapko jannati pari milega. And all this is taught in madrassas. But at least teach your children that they are Indian. It is not tolerable that you will burst crackers when Pakistan wins.

Q) Abhi in logon ko 2002 ke baad kam nahi hua?

A) Haan abhi thoda kam hua hai.

Q) So you spend about eight hours in court?

A) What to do? I am losing my practice. But they can't save me from court because there are 80 others. People like Teesta will start shouting.

Q) But tell me something, there is a lot of pschophancy around Narendra Modi, isn't it? I mean all the good work is credited to him?

A) It is good now, but for the long run it's bad.

Q) Are you one of his favourites?

A) I was a favourite.

Q) At least if nothing, the Gujaratis will not forget what you did for them?

A) They will never forget that. They stand by me.

Q) What is happening with Modi post that Amit Shah thing?

A) I haven't spoken to him post my arrest and bail. We have met twice I think on two occasions.

Q) So how does he react when he sees you?

A) He does not react, does not say anything. And even I don't. Anyway it is my problem I will handle it. God will help me. Why should I expect any help from anybody.

I know I am innocent and God will help me. I was not there Maithili, I was 20 kms away from that place. I was at Sola. I went to the assembly, which started at 8.30. I went there. I started from my house, went to Anandiben's office. We went there. We chatted there.

Q) So, Anandiben should also have been questioned no?

A) I don't know. From there I went to the hospital, because all the dead bodies were at Sola civil hospital. My nurse's father was a victim of Godhra and I had gone there to identify his body. Amit Shah and I went to the civil hospital. Even Hindus tortured me there, they were angry. They shouted against me and Amit Shah. PI escorted me to his own car and he took me [away].

Q) So what's the allegation?

A) They are using witnesses to prove that I was instigating riots. That I was leading the mob. I came to my hospital…attended a labour patient. 3oclock I went to the hospital.They said that the mobile was there in this particular locality so I was there.

Q) Gordhan Zadaphia was Home Minister. He was also removed for the same reason?

A) No, he was removed because he was not in the good books of the CM.

Q) So the CM didn't use witnesses like he used in the Amit Shah case to save Gordhanbhai?

A) No [laughs].

Q) So he also got rid of Gordhan Zadaphia because of the riots?

A) Yes, he went.

Q) So, it became a good way for him to eliminate people he didn't like?

A) Yes.

Q) What's with this Amit Shah?

A) He's his man, very close to him.

Q) I thought Anandiben was more his person.

A) Anandiben is the right hand and he is the left. He did every possible thing to get Amit Shah out. Advani came down to meet him. Sushma Swaraj went down to his residence.

Q) But that wasn't done when you were arrested?

A) What to do. Anyway there's God there.

Looks like he will be portrayed as the PM candidate. Aur usko takkar dene waala bhi koi nahi hai..He will make Anandiben the CM.

Q) Ye sab log kitna bolte hain unke peeche. Ye aapke encounter cops bhi yahi bolte hain ki use and throw kiya?

A) Haan, Vanzara bahut achcha tha. Dekho encounters toh kiya in logon ne, lekin jo sahi wajah hai, the reason why the encounters happened ye kyun nahi saamne aa raha. Jaise ki Sohrabuddin ko maara terrorist bolke, uski wife ko kyun maara, who toh terrorist nahi thi naa. That Kausar Bi. He was bad person, you can encounter him, but why his wife?

Q) Haren Pandya and Gordhan Zadaphia dono ko nikal diya na?

A) Gordhanbhai toh theek the, Haren Pandya was a very dynamic man

Q) Lekin Gordhanbhai ko bhi toh riots mein use karke phenk diya isne?

A) Yes, yes.

There were riots in all of Gujarat, but they were after the Naroda MLA, me.

Q) Made you into a scapegoat?

A) Yes.

Q) So what happened in the Modi interrogation?

A) He also went to the SIT but he has been let off.

Q) But by the benchmark used against you, he too should have been arrested?

A) haha...[nods].

Q) I am meeting him tomorrow, your Modi?

A) When you meet Modi, ask him why is he such a controversial man?

Q) Really?

A) He turns everything in his favour.

Q) So did these people come to meet you in jail?

A) No, none of them.

Q) So, you could go behind bars any day?

A) Yes any day, any day, once the judgement comes in.

Q) What should I ask Modi, now he will dodge [my questions]?

A) You should twist the question around when you meet him. Praise him and then ask him....

Q) About you?

A) Ask him in some other way, ask him why some of his ministers are involved.

Ask P.C.Pande, he knows everything, he knows the truth. Ask him, he was the Commissioner of Ahmedabad.

Q) So why doesn't he speak the truth?

A) I don't know.

Q) Now I know why his face fell [when asked about Kodnani].

A) Why should he bother talking about me now.

Q) What about Modi?

A) Praise him and his style of working, and then he will talk. You know what he will tell you, trademark answer, 'I love Vivekananda, I love Sardar Vallabh bhai Patel'. Ask him about me and he will say 'Achcha hum kya karein, SIT was there, phone call records the' or he will just give a short and sweet answer 'the matter is subjudice'.

Q) Then all these points apply to him too?

A) Haha...ask him that.

Q) By the way, I was supposed to meet Jayanti Ravi, and I didn't realize, she was there during Godhra?

A) Oh yes, Jayanti Ravi, she was the Godhra collector, the officer in charge. At that time she was in the line of fire for not allowing Anandiben to do any riots. So then she was not in the good books of the government. Now she's back. Details I don't know. Also don't tell him that you know me or that you have met me when you meet him, because he will keep that in mind.

There is no doubt about the rumours that Maya Kodnani complained to the RSS that she was convicted while Modi was let off by the SIT. There is no ambiguity that Maya Kodnani not just believed that Amit Shah was close to Modi but also that Modi would go to any extreme to save Shah. During her conversation with me, she reasserted the facts I had heard many times before that officers were used and then abandoned as per convenience.

Geeta Johri

I woke up Paani early that morning, she was needed. Paani was barely 18, and back in Greenland she used to work as a confectionary chef. She wore the most interesting clothes. She was the life of the party at the Foundation. Her face would light up every time we would play 'Sheela ki jawaani' and she would start an impromptu jig. She even did this once at Mumbai airport when we were leaving for Ahmedabad. I had a plan in mind but was not convinced about whether Paani would be able to help me. All she would be enthused about was the latest jazz number she was listening to on that day.

I asked her out for a smoke on the terrace and checked with her if she would be interested in a day-long trip to Rajkot. I had a meeting that would last an hour and I needed her help, I told her. 'Are we going by bus?' she asked excited at the prospect. Yes, I said, a six-hour-long journey and we would be checking into a hotel. I also needed Paani's assistance for another purpose. Her passport. In Ahmedabad I had somehow managed accommodation but for a Rajkot hotel I would need the necessary authentication and Paani would be of immense help with regard to that.

The next morning we took the bus to Rajkot. I was equipped with my cameras and a backpack full of chips, my laptop, music and chocolates. When the bus stopped for refreshments Paani headed straight for the lassi seller. The bus was full of men, mostly traders, so when Paani lit her cigarette, she attracted quite a bit of attention. I held her hand throughout as if to shield her from unwanted attention. Till the time that we returned to Ahmedabad, Paani was my responsibility. I felt a strange kind of kinship with her. She was like the little sister I had never had.

When we reached the hotel, Paani's passport did the needful. I was registered as Maithili and she entered the room letting out a squeal of excitement. The bathroom had a bathtub and the glass window gave her a view of the entire city. She was thrilled and I was nervous. Geeta Johri, one of the most controversial officers of the time had given me an appointment. I had spoken to her about profiling her as a woman achiever and also sent her a fake script.

When we went to meet Johri, she welcomed us into her room telling me that she had been waiting for us with great excitement. She was posted as the Commissioner of Rajkot and it was not difficult for us to locate her. She took to Paani within minutes who animatedly described her bus ride. Johri then exclaimed that I seemed to have become a total firang after having spent eight years in America. 'You have such a heavy accent.' She spoke about her daughter who was abroad and how very often her friends would visit and stay with them in Rajkot. She offered to have Paani stay at her home the next time she visited and Paani agreed immediately. I nodded for the moment. This was no time for any disagreement. I could explain things to Paani later.

I began by talking about all the accounts of her bravery and then expressed surprise that one of the reports had something negative to say about her. 'Oh, it's the Sohrabuddin encounter, you wouldn't know much about it.

It was a killing for which all officials in Gujarat are under scrutiny.'

Oh yes, I told her with my eyes wide open, every officer I visit talks about this case. She laughed at how a 'ruffian' had held the state hostage. This was the same Geeta Johri who, according to her junior V.L.Solanki, had asked for the status report, that was to be sent to the Supreme Court on the Sohrabuddin fake encounter, to be changed. It was in a meeting at Amit Shah's residence that she had been asked to change the details in the report. The Supreme Court while handing over the CBI investigation had reprimanded Geeta Johri for mishandling the investigation.

It is essential at this point in time for the reader to know Geeta Johri a little more intimately.

Geeta Johri, of the 1982 batch, was Gujarat's first woman IPS officer. Her career graph had seen many ups and downs since the 1990s. In September 1992, Johri catapulted to fame when she took on mafia don Abdul Latif by raiding his den in Popatiawad at Dariapur and arrested his gunman Sharif Khan. But Latif managed to escape.

In 2006, while on a posting with CID(crime), she headed the investigations into the Sohrabuddin Sheikh fake encounter and the killing of his wife Kausarbi, following a petition filed by Sohrabuddin's brother Rubabuddin in the Supreme Court. Her detailed and rigorous inquiry confirmed that the encounter was a fake one. The inquiry also exposed the involvement of several police officers and on the basis of the evidence gathered by her, 13 police officers were arrested, including controversial DIG DG

Vanzara, SP Rajkumar Pandian and Dinesh MN. The arrests were made by DIG Police, Rajnish Rai, who was formally in-charge of the investigation.

Soon, Rai was asked to quit the probe and Johri was reinstated. But before leaving, Rai handed over the CDs containing the telephone records of the three accused to his superiors. Johri had a major showdown with her superiors and was then asked to report directly to the apex court. However, the chargesheet that she filed before the sessions court in the case was severely criticized. The SC ordered that the case be transferred to the CBI after finding faults in Johri's handling of the case.

Johri was the most crucial element in the fake encounters case. I had in an oped stated earlier that, 'In an ideal world and in ideal circumstances Geeta Johri would have been a role model for women who aspired to be in the services. But neither is it an ideal world nor did luck favour Geeta Johri.'

I began my conversation with her by enquiring if everything was fine, as she was looking quite stressed.

A) I was going through a very rough patch last couple of months...things were very bad.

Q) When these controversies started, were you anticipating them?

A) Sometimes you don't expect them. I wasn't, there was no reason for me to have anticipated them. Especially when you are doing a good job, you don't expect anybody to find anything wrong. But things go wrong at times due to reasons, sometimes they are political.

Q) Yours was more political?

A) Yes, mine was more political. Different set of government, different governments in the state and centre.

Q) I have been reading a lot about you. I was told you almost stalled the Parliament.

A) Haha, yes that Sohrabuddin case. There were some nasty press reports. Media reports said all nasty things about me.

Q) So you are saying that the CBI never wanted to arrest you?

A) No, the CBI never said that it wanted to arrest me. I was in London at that point of time, undergoing training and I kept on hearing about this. When I came back I saw all these press reports. I mean if you have got evidence you present it. That's what I asked them .This is all off the record alright!

So they basically asked me about the Home Minister. Now I never saw eye to eye with the Home Minister so I told them that I never saw eye to eye with Amit Shah when the CBI asked me about it. And nobody, no politician talks to me because they are really scared of me. You know nobody has called me in the last two years.

Q) Is it the same Home Minister?

A) Yes, Home Minister Amit Shah, it may be ridiculous but I never wanted to speak to him. It was just a threat they were giving me.

My husband has been a pillar of support. He has

been with me through thick and thin, he helps me draft all the applications. He's the forest officer, based in Gandhinagar.

Q) Everybody has been talking of this encounter... the Sohrabuddin encounter? Interesting case.

A) More than him, his wife Kausar Bi. She was an old woman, I mean she had two kids. Both teenagers. She must have been around 35 or 40. She was already married to somebody else. She had gone to Indore to be with her sister, her sister used to run a beauty salon and that's where she fell in love with this Sohrabuddin. They got married, she got a divorce from her husband.

He's a criminal, an extortionist.

Q) And because of a criminal a state went into an upheaval?

A) Well he was a criminal and they wanted to kill Sohrabuddin in an encounter but they did it foolishly. They picked him up from a bus full of people. You don't do that. These are things supposed to be done in a clandestine manner, not so openly. This is how they got caught.

Q) And hence the woman also got encountered ?

A) No, she refused to leave him because she realised that they will encounter him. When they killed him they realized that Kausar Bi will speak out so they killed her. So basically the issue was not that Sohrabuddin got encountered, the issue was that Kausar Bi was killed.

Sohrabuddin looked genuine. Kausar Bi's family got a whiff and went to the Supreme Court.

At that point of time I was with the CID crime. So the Supreme Court decided to send that case to us. I guess me being a woman and [it was a] woman who went missing hence the case came to me. So I went about finding her.

Then the whole thing started. Then it turned out to be more political. Kausar Bi and Sohrabuddin everybody forgot.

Q) Why was the Home Minister involved?

A) Because they came out with this that it was illegally directed, illegally killed. Sohrabuddin got killed and Kausar bi was killed and when you start investigating everything comes out. That [it] must have been done at the behest of the Home Minister. But there was no direct evidence. 13 police officers I had arrested, that was a lot you know, it was like working against the tide, working against the state, the roughest patch.

Q) Working against your own people?

A) Yes.

Q) But the government would have put so much pressure on you?

A) Yes, everybody did, my own colleagues. And the internal conflict, but at the end of it, even I didn't subscribe to Sohrabuddin, but there are ways, you have to do things in a seemingly legal manner, at least on paper you have to make it look seemingly legally correct.

Q) That must have been a hell of a time for you?

A) Yes, I was not very convinced, comfortable in arresting the officers at least in the Sohrabuddin case. Kausar Bi, I was convinced.

Q) The HM was not arrested then?

A) No I did not arrest him because if you are arresting your own men you go by pure evidence.

Q) But the CBI arrested him?

A) The CBI arrested only the HM and one more officer. 13 were arrested by me. They did not arrest any other person or have put one item more in it. They arrested the HM on legally flimsy evidence and I didn't.

Many people insist that Johri, who was initially doing a fine job with the fake encounters case, was blackmailed with certain corruption cases that were linked to her husband.[23] A note which was presented to the CBI said that her husband Anil who was an IFS officer was the reason she obfuscated the process of investigation and saved Amit Shah from the case. But it is still baffling that a police officer who rode into the den of a noted gangster in an auto could have been made to buckle via blackmail. That there was a concerted effort to save Amit Shah especially after Geeta Johri wrote of pressure from the CBI spoke volumes. Incidentally, days before the CBI was to question Geeta Johri again, Arun Jaitley, then the leader of opposition in the Rajya Sabha

---

23 http://www.tehelka.com/2010/09/geeta-johri-was-known-to-be-a-fearless-officer-so-what-accounts-for-her-flip-flops/?singlepage=1

wrote a long letter to the then Prime Minister Manmohan Singh[24] on 27 September 2013. This extract from the letter is particularly interesting:

> The Congress strategy in the face of its depleting popularity is clear. Congress cannot fight the BJP and Narendra Modi politically. Defeat stares them in the face. By misuse of investigative agencies they have so far tried various methods of falsely implicating Narendra Modi, the Chief Minister of Gujarat, Shri Amit Shah, the then Home Minister and also the Minister of Law, Transport & Parliamentary Affairs of the State of Gujarat and General Secretary of Bhartiya Janata Party and other important BJP leaders.

This letter from Arun Jaitley was published just two weeks after D.G.Vanzara who was behind bars for seven years for the Sohrabuddin and Tulsi Prajapti fake encounters cases and later an accused in the Ishrat Jahan fake encounter case wrote a letter accusing Amit Shah of treachery.[25] He wrote that Shah had ensured that all cops arrested in the case were languishing in jail while he manipulated the judiciary to keep himself out of trouble. In his letter, Vanzara had summarized the sentiments of officers like Girish Singhal who accused the Modi-Shah duo of a use-and-throw policy. He wrote,

With the passage of time, I realized that this government

---

24 http://www.dnaindia.com/india/report-arun-jaitley-writes-to-pm-on-congress-dirty-war-against-narendra-modi-1896969

25 http://www.ndtv.com/cheat-sheet/jailed-cop-dg-vanzara-attacks-amit-shah-gujarat-government-over-fake-encounters-533486

was not only not interested in protecting us but it also has been clandestinely making all efforts to keep me and my officers in the jail so as to save its own skin from CBI on one hand and gain political benefits on the other. It is everybody's knowledge that this government has been reaping very rich political dividends, since last 12 years, by keeping the glow of encounter cases alive in the sky of Gujarat, while otherwise, remaining in the low profile and indifferent to the fate of jailed police officers.

With all regards for Hon'ble Supreme Court of India, I sincerely believe and state that but for the legal and political intrigues, machinations and maneuverings of Shri Amitbhai Shah, the trial of Shohrabuddin encounter case, followed by that of Tulasiram Prajapati would not have gone out of the state of Gujarat. I would like to state in the most unambiguous words that this government, through the dirty tactics of Shri Amitbhai Shah, is unfortunately managing only for its own self so as to swim and continue to prosper in all directions, while ditching the police officers so as to sink and allow them to die unnatural death by drowning. I have been maintaining my graceful silence for such a long period only and only because of my supreme faith in and highest respect for Shri Narendrabhai Modi, Hon'ble Chief Minister of Gujarat, whom I used to adore like a God. But, I am sorry to state that my God could not rise to the occasion under the evil influence of Shri Amitbhai Shah who usurped his eyes and ears and has been successfully misguiding him by converting goats into dogs and dogs into goats since last 12 years. His unholy grip over the state administration is so complete that he is almost running the government of Gujarat by proxy.

The letter dominated news headlines as here the very man who had once been so close to both Narendra Modi and Amit Shah was now accusing them of conspiracy promising to reveal more in the days to follow. Within days another absconding cop ex-DG P.P. Pande who was an accused in the Ishrat Jahan case appeared and promised to speak to the media as well on the matter.

Within months of the BJP coming to power at the centre in Delhi, bail was granted to D.G.Vanzara and he was given a hero's welcome in Gujarat. Other officers like Rajkumar Pandian and Abhay Chudasama who had been arrested as two of the main accused in the Sohrabuddin case are now out on bail and have been reinstated by the Gujarat police. Earlier this year the CBI dropped all charges against Geeta Johri who was promoted to DGP of Police Gujarat. The wheels of justice in all cases in Gujarat clearly seemed to have turned backwards.

Haren Pandya

While reporting for *Tehelka* in Mumbai, in 2008 I had met Mumbai encounter cop Daya Nayak on several occasions. Daya is quite a character and last I checked he did not wish to speak to me because I had mentioned his alleged involvement in the Sadiq Jamal fake encounter case in Gujarat. The CBI had questioned him and Pradeep Sharma extensively, both of whom had to be suspended. At one point both Daya Nayak and Pradeep Sharma were the most high-profile cops in Mumbai. Filmmaker Ram Gopal Verma even made a film *Ab tak chappan* about these two cops. They were eulogised, and were the toast of society circles till they were finally caught on the wrong side of the law.

Daya had many friends in the media or rather he was very media savvy. He would be a regular at the Costa cafe or Café Coffee Day at Lokhandwala Market where his friends from the gym would come and say hello to him. Nayak loved to flaunt his revolver which was always tucked into his trousers. During one of my meetings with him in 2008 when my colleague and I were working on a series on the misuse of MCOCA, the draconian terror law in Maharashtra, Nayak said something that stayed with me. The biggest political murder in the country, he said, had happened in Gujarat, that of Haren Pandya, Modi's arch rival. I asked him if he had proof. He said, 'You are the journalist, it's your job to investigate.' We left the conversation at that.

Once back home I had tried to read up every possible story on the Haren Pandya assassination. There had been an element of doubt ever since Pandya was assassinated by alleged Muslim men. But Pandya's father Vitthal Pandya, maintained till his last breath that his son had been murdered by his political rivals in Gujarat. His wife Jagruti Pandya who had contested the elections in Gujarat had also said that the CM and Amit Shah were involved in Pandya's

murder.[26] But her claim had been taken as a manifestation
of the anguish that the grief-stricken family members were
feeling.

One story in this regard that was clear in my memory
was coincidentally an investigative report written by senior
journalist Sankarshan Thakur. I am briefly recounting here
many findings from Sankarshan's brilliant reportage.

Yaadram, the lone eyewitness, says he was too dazed by
what he saw to even move from the spot for an hour; when
he does move, he informs not the police but his seth, a
local businessman called Snehal Adenwala. Adenwala does
not inform the police either, although he knows the man
lying dead in the Maruti 800 in the Law Gardens parking
lot is Haren Pandya; he calls Pandya's associate, Prakash
Shah, and tells him instead. Shah, too, does not call the
police. He calls Pandya's secretary Neelesh Bhatt, who is
at Pandya's house, already worrying about why his boss is
late returning. It is then that Bhatt rushes to Law Gardens,
locates the car and opens it to find his boss repeatedly
shot. This is at a little past 10. Gujarat's former minister of
state for home has been lying dead in a car in the centre
of town for more than two hours.

Meantime, the Ellisbridge police receive another call
from the control room — find out what's happening at
Law Gardens, there's a commotion, there are rumours.

26 http://indiatoday.intoday.in/story/jagruti-haren-pandyas-wife-
   to-contest-gujarat-polls-keshubhai-patel-gujarat-parivartan-
   party/1/235242.html

Now another SI, YA Shaikh, heads out. Midway to Law Gardens, Shaikh gets another control room call — go to Parimal Gardens, not Law Gardens; he changes course. At 10:50, he gets yet another call, this time to head to Law Gardens. He lands there at 10:54, nearly three hours after Pandya might have been shot. And guess what? Shaikh's colleague, SI Naik, who started for Law Gardens ahead of him, still hasn't reached the spot. Who was ordering the local police about that morning? Why such delay in getting to a spot that is no more than ten minutes away?

The post-mortem, conducted at the VS Hospital the same afternoon, reveals Pandya sustained seven bullet injuries. From five bullets. Five of these injuries are 0.8cm in diameter, two are 0.5cm. It is scientifically possible for the same firearm to cause different-sized wounds because of surface tension and resistance. It is also possible for five bullets to leave seven injuries because bullets can travel through body parts. But independent experts who have examined the case closely maintain that it is highly unlikely in this case. Two bullets, in other words, have not been traced.

The bullet that caused injury number 5 on the post-mortem report was fired into the lower part of Pandya's scrotum and travelled upwards into his chest, piercing his abdominal wall. Is it possible for a man sitting in a car — and a heavyset six-foot-plus man like Pandya in a small Maruti 800 at that — to be shot through the scrotum? Any man shot through his scrotum, as Pandya was, is going to bleed profusely; the scrotum is an intricate web of blood vessels that control body temperature. Did Pandya bleed? Yes. Are there traces in the car? No. Pandya was shot through his scrotum, his neck, twice through his chest, once through his arm. The car should have been drenched, or at least his seat should have been. Yet forensic reports find no evidence of blood in the vehicle, save for a dab on the front passenger seat and another on the key chain (Central Forensic Sciences Laboratory report no. CFSL-2003/F-0232).

Forensic reports also do not record any gunshot residue inside Pandya's car (report of Mobile Forensic Science Laboratory, Gujarat State). Five bullets, if not more, were fired into him, apparently while he sat in the car. Yet no bullet residue?

Was Haren Pandya shot in his car at all? Or did the murder happen elsewhere and was his body planted in the car later? Where did Pandya go after he left home that morning? There are clues that could help find out. But they have vanished or become unavailable.

When Pandya's body was taken out of the car at Law Gardens, he was wearing shoes; by the time he was taken in for post-mortem, the shoes were gone, there's no record of them. The shoes could contain vital clues to where Pandya went that morning.

Pandya's cellphone, a grey, fliptop Samsung, was recovered

by the police from the car. The police either did not care to check or is hiding the call data records from Pandya's phone that day. These could tell who Pandya called or was called by; these calls could, again, be a vital link in getting to the truth. But the records aren't there. When Pandya's mobile service provider, Hutch, was asked for the records, it produced manifests from January and February of 2003. For records of March 2003, it took a strange plea: they are too old, Hutch pleaded. But surely, January and February come before March.

Could the strange case of Mufti Sufian, an accused in the case, be a part of that cutout? Sufian is a young cleric who made a quick name for himself making incendiary speeches at Ahmedabad's Lal Masjid. It is known that he had become more hardline following the 2002 violence, fanning counter-communal flames during his post-prayer discourses. It is also known he had links with Ahmedabad's underworld which lives off bootlegging. Sufian is alleged to have played a role in contracting Asghar Ali for the Pandya hit. Within a week of the murder, while he was apparently still under watch, Sufian slipped out of the country. Where to? Nobody knows. Bangladesh, Pakistan, Afghanistan, Yemen, nobody quite knows. The CBI elevated Sufian to the rogues' gallery on it's website and had Interpol post a red-corner notice for him. He was, on paper, a wanted man, accused of the conspiracy to murder Pandya. Yet, a year or so after Sufian's mysterious escape, his wife and children managed to vaporise as well. 'They should have been under strict watch, they were the last clue we had to Sufian's whereabouts,' says a senior police officer, and yet they got away. How could that be possible? Did someone help them out? Did Sufian hold uncomfortable secrets? Was there a deal?

The first time I met Jagruti Pandya was in 2010, a little before I began my sting. And when I was still investigating the Sohrabuddin encounters. I had only seen her as a spirited woman on TV following her husband's death demanding a fair probe. She lived with her two sons and her father in an upper-middle-class locality in Ahmedabad. There was something very brave about Jagrutiben or Jagrutiji as I began to call her later. Today I can call her a dear friend whose brave struggle to find her husband's killers needs a standing ovation. Haren Pandya was a favourite of the RSS and L.K.Advani and many other BJP leaders, besides being a favourite of various police officers in Gujarat. While his role in the Gujarat riots is allegedly controversial, it is believed that many from the Muslim community were also fond of him.

There was a sense of bitterness in Jagrutiji for Muslims as one of them had allegedly killed her husband. As luck would have it, she chose to believe that Rana was a Hindu name. I found it very embarrassing to correct her and decided I would let her find out what my faith was once she came across my surname in one of my columns later. Every time she spoke about her husband's assassins she would refer to Muslims as 'these people' and at times she would call them 'a violent lot'. But from the moment I met Jagrutiben her conviction that the Muslim boys were 'used' by somebody powerful baffled me. Here was a woman who had lost her husband eight years ago. Her younger son had almost no memory even of his father's funeral. Yet, besides making sure that her sons received a disciplined upbringing, she did not give up on her fight for justice, making sure however, that it never affected her children adversely. Her younger son is a state-level sportsman and her older son works for a private firm. Both stood by their mother like a rock without any doubt about her conviction that there was a larger conspiracy at work that caused their father's death. Jagrutiji had pertinent questions about her husband's death based on the phone call records which she gave me, and the details of Mufti Sufiyan and his family whom she tried to meet.[27]

She had also brought up the detailed report by Sankarshan Thakur (referred to and excerpted from above) with me. I met her right after Amit Shah was sent behind bars and when details emerged about Tulsi Prajapati (who was also killed in a fake encounter) having held critical information about Pandya's murder. In October 2011, months after I had returned to Delhi following my sting operation I wrote an article about Pandya's killing in which I asked some important questions:

---

27 Mufti Sufiyan was the mastermind of the assassination and a local priest who had conveniently escaped from Gujarat after Pandya was killed. It was interesting that despite living right next to the police headquarters in Ahmedabad, he had found it easy to escape within a week of Pandya's death.

Why is it that Sufiyan's father praises Chudasama, who was then with the Ahmedabad Crime Branch? Why did Chudasama promise the family, if his father is to be believed, that no harm would come to them? While the CBI, which was handed over the initial probe by the Crime Branch, claims it had a watertight case, a logical question that could be asked is: Why could the CBI team investigating the case not send a letter rogatory for tracing Sufiyan?

Second, the CBI investigating officer claims that Pandya's call records of March 2003 could not be found, while those of the two previous months were provided. These records, a copy of which is with TEHELKA, show 40 calls made by a female journalist from Ahmedabad. Surprisingly, neither the CBI nor the police quizzed her. Third, prime witness Anil Yadram, who runs a food cart near Law Garden and had allegedly witnessed the murder, has given contradictory statements. He told the police that he was too confused to react but an hour later called the owner of his cart, who in turned called Pandya's associate – but not the police. When TEHELKA met Yadram, he gave three contradictory statements on all three days. On Day 1, he said Ali came on a bike; Day 2, he said he saw him walk towards the car; Day 3, he did not remember the chain of events. Fourth, as per the forensic report, there were six holes in Pandya's kurta. But only five bullets were found in his body. If he was sitting behind the steering wheel and the weapon was fired from the right window, which was part-open, he should not have suffered any wound in the scrotum. The prosecution explained and the judge accepted that he fell sideways on the passenger seat, but this seems improbable. And fifth, an FIR filed by the police control room log showed confusion or delay. With these loopholes and the changing stance of witnesses, it was only natural that the HC, in a shocking move, acquitted all 12 accused in the case last month and also ruled that there was no evidence to prove that Ali had shot Pandya.

I met Jagrutiben on many occasions later; we would go on drives, or out for dinner. She had found a confidante, and I had found a friend who gave me the strength to uncover the truth. I remember once meeting Jagrutiben to get the chargesheet filed in the case of her husband's murder. It was the month of Ramzaan and I was fasting. The moment I entered the house, she offered me some nimbu paani. I declined saying I could not. She offered to make me tea. 'No Jagrutiben, ramzaan hai na, mera roza hai. Kuch kha pee nahi sakti,' I told her. She looked stunned then and somehow managed to put together a few words. 'Aap Mohammedan ho? Mujhe pata nahi tha,' she said, almost embarrassed at the thought of having used uncharitable words for my community so many times in my presence. 'Koi baat nahi, aapki jagah main hoti toh mujhse bhi bhool ho sakti thi. Aapke saath jo hua hai woh koi muaaf nahi kar sakta,' I reassured her.

She sat with me going through the pages of the

chargesheet and call records and diligently answered my questions.

She explained that her husband had deposed before the VR Krishna Iyer-led citizens' inquiry into the Gujarat genocide of 2002. It was a secretly arranged deposition, but she believed Modi had found out about it. Modi had various prestige issues with Haren, she insisted, which is why he disobeyed the BJP high command and forced her husband to vacate his Ellisbridge seat. Pandya, she said, had become a political thorn for Narendra Modi as he had always been in the good books of the RSS and enjoyed their patronage.

When I started getting ready to leave, she asked me where I was staying in Ahmedabad. At around 6.30 in the evening on the same day, about 30 minutes before iftaar(breaking of the fast), she called me. She was standing outside my hotel, waiting to take me to an eatery where I could break my fast.

From that day on Jagrutiben became extremely protective about me. I know this state, she told me. You are working so hard to uncover the truth about my husband. It is my duty to protect you, especially with the surname you carry.

There were too many officials involved in the Haren Pandya investigation. CBI officials had taken over the case within days of the murder and the FIR as per protocol was prepared and signed by the Gujarat police. I went through the FIR—the investigating officer was an inspector called Y.A.Shaikh (also mentioned in the news report above).

Coincidentally he was a friend of V.L.Solanki (who has been referred to earlier with respect to Geeta Johri).

Sheikh did not meet visitors and most certainly not media persons. I had not begun my sting operation yet and was in Ahmedabad after Shah's arrest trying to do my research. I met V.L.Solanki twice who after doing a background check on me asked me to reach his residence. Outside his home was a police jeep with police constables in it who provided extra security to him after he gave the statement against Geeta Johri.

Solanki stood by every word that he had said to the CBI. And then just before I was leaving I casually asked Solanki if he knew of an officer called Sheikh. 'Why do you want to meet him or know about him?' he reacted sharply. 'Just thought I would meet him about a case,' I retorted mildly. He smiled and then escorted me out of the house saying, 'Rehne do ben, woh nahi milega aapse, aur aap ye sab mein mat pado.'

Sheikh was scared of his colleagues and of the state because he had filed the FIR in the Pandya case. He was the one who was involved in the investigation before it was transferred to the CBI after Pandya's father complained that there was more to the case which was being suppressed.

There was a lawyer in Gujarat who knew Sheikh well and to whom Sheikh often went for advice. I requested him to arrange one single meeting with Sheikh. I asked him to play the religion card if need be saying that I was a Muslim sympathetic to cops like him who were feeling suffocated under the current dispensation.

At that time, I was staying at the Ambassador Hotel in Khanpur, a Muslim-dominated area. Every morning and evening the azaan from the local mosque helped me in eating my sehri and iftaar during Ramzaan. Ambassador was owned by a Sindhi businessman. Right opposite Ambassador was a restaurant that was run by a Muslim with others from the community frequenting the place right after breaking the fast for tea and savouries.

This was the place where Sheikh agreed to meet me for the first time. I introduced myself, told him that I was the journalist who had provided the evidence in the Sohrabuddin and Tulsi Prajapati cases that had sent Amit Shah behind bars. He told me I didn't need to explain as all of Gujarat knew of a man called Rana Ayyub. I laughed.

Sheikh appeared very apprehensive. I reassured him that I was a devout, practising Muslim and how much I felt for those who had been killed in the riots. He responded meekly, 'Aap *Tehelka* waale ho, dar lagta hai aap logon se baat karna, pata nahi kya record kar loge.'

I asked him to check my diary and my bag, and he laughed in embarrassment. I offered to meet him again and did not communicate with him at all through the next week.

It worked; the following week I met Sheikh again, this time to break his trust. It broke me from within, the guilt killed me. He knew who I was. I was Rana Ayyub the journalist who would keep all information confidential. But here was a man who possibly knew the truth. It had been 10 years since Pandya's killing and there was no hope of any headway in the case. I thought of carrying my spy cam and recording his conversation but to use it only when nothing else came my way. After my meeting with

Sheikh I made every possible effort to find that one bit of evidence. I even visited Mufti Sufiyan's residence but all they would do was praise the cops. They had clearly been tutored well.

Sheikh spoke openly when we met the next time.

A) Before I begin, let me tell you something. You are being shadowed by the IB. The highest authority in the IB?

Q) State IB or Central IB?

A) State IB. He told me that you were visiting me. They have come to know that you visited me so they have asked me to be careful. That is their job... so I am telling you to be careful.

Q) But why would they be against me?

A) You know this Haren Pandya case is like a volcano. Once the truth is out, Modi will go home. He will be jailed, not go home. He will be in prison. Look at this, two days after Jagruti Pandya's plea to look into Azam Khan's statement in the Haren Pandya case, he was shot at in Udaipur. He survived so he was threatened and politically pressurized.

Q) But I am really intrigued. How did the IB come to know about me?

A) Madam, because the IB works for Mr Modi.
Why don't you sting the witness Anil Yadram?

Q) But why, what will he have to say?

A) Arre, he will say the real story, who approached him first, what he knew and what he was asked to say. Chudasama was also involved in this case. He is hand-in-glove with many criminals.

Chudasama and all the officers are doing all this with inspectors like Barot. Barot is the inspector, low-level guy, he does all the paperwork.

Q) Why did the witness Anil Yadram give a wrong statement?

A) Madam, they tutored him in custody. They had Asghar Ali in custody before the assassination so they tutored him.

After the assassination of Mr Pandya they wanted to plant Asghar Ali, and they needed a witness.

Q) Why did they have to keep Asghar in detention?

A) They had to put the blame on any Muslim henchman. He was in illegal detention. What will he say later in his defence?

And you don't need Asghar Ali's confession. All they need is evidence.

Q) So are you saying that Tarun Barot, Chudasama and Vanzara were complicit in this?

A) Yes.

Kanhaiyya just narrated that he was going in a car and he saw Haren Pandya lying in a car.

Sushil Gupta the CBI officer approved the concocted story of the Gujarat police. Gupta resigned from the CBI, he is now a lawyer with the SC. He's on the payroll of Reliance. Ask him why did he resign from the CBI. He sits in the Supreme Court. Meet him.

Q) So the CBI did not do its investigation.

A) It just did patch up. It bought the entire theory given by the Gujarat police officers.

Q) Is it a political murder?

A) Everybody was involved. It was at Advani's behest that the case was handed over to the CBI. Because he was Narendra Modi's mentor. So to clear him, I mean, people will not buy the story of the local police but they will buy the story of CBI.

Mufti ran much later.

Q) Whose role was there? Barot or Vanzara?

A) All three.

Barot was somewere else and Chudasama was brought on deputation. They had got Chudasama. He works for the government. There is a Porbander connection in this encounter. It's a blind case. They have just fit Asghar Ali and the witness. The investigation was done by the Crime Branch and nobody believed the investigation. Not even Vitthal Pandya.

Q) Why did CBI buy it?

A) The CBI rescued Modi in this case.

As we say, some statements do not need any explanation. The man who allegedly shot Haren Pandya, Asghar Ali is in a prison in Hyderabad. The other boys who were arrested were from Andhra Pradesh and also had connections with those involved in the Tulsi Prajapati and Sohrabuddin killings. So who exactly killed Haren Pandya? Was Sheikh indulging in hearsay? The question is why would he? He was the investigating officer who had signed the relevant papers. He was the one who had conducted the initial investigation followed by Abhay Chudasama who was later arrested by the CBI.

Why were Sohrabuddin and Prajapati killed? Till date the motive is not very clear. Why is it that Mufti Sufiyan who was the mastermind of the Haren Pandya assassination according to the CBI chargesheet managed an easy escape from the state to a neighbouring country? Why was Sufiyan's family so thankful to Abhay Chudasama who is chargesheeted for having fixed innocents in fake cases?

Haren Pandya, one of the most loved Home Ministers of Gujarat had allegedly expressed his desire to appear before a citizen's tribunal in the Gujarat riots case. Is the truth hidden somewhere in this offer? It is time we blew the lid off this maze of injustice and conflicting evidence.

CHAPTER 11

Disclosure

I had moved back to Mumbai post the investigation and right after got a call from P.C.Pande if I had wrapped up research on my film. He suggested that I meet the CM. I jumped at the opportunity. I sent a mail to my seniors and Shoma and Tarun gave me an immediate go-ahead. They also arranged for Mike to be sent to Ahmedabad one last time to assist me. Mike's parents were in Delhi to visit him but he somehow found an excuse to be in Ahmedabad for a day.

I had explained to Mike that there would be strict frisking at the CM's residence and we had to go there because not doing so would invite P.C.Pande's suspicion. For the sake of record, I wore my watch which had a camera attached to it. We had taken a local tourist car that day. Since I was no longer staying at the Foundation at this point, I had again asked for the keys of that desolate bungalow on SG Highway for a day. Mike and I had reached Modi's Gandhinagar residence an hour early. So we asked our driver to park our car close by while we waited for the clock to tick faster. I was nervous while Mike kept smiling. My concern was that if the camera in my watch caught the attention of the security check and the metal barriers, we were done for. Half an hour later when we walked into the CM's residence I breathed easy when I walked through security without being caught.

Modi's OSD Sanjay Bhavsar met us. We were finally escorted to the CM's room. He stood up to greet us. Mike exclaimed that he had seen his posters in the autos in Ahmedabad and was very impressed with his popularity. On the table were two books on Barack Obama. 'So will you be the next PM sir?' I asked immediately. He blushed and started to speak about Barack Obama who was his inspiration and the virtues of Swami Vivekananda. After a 30-minute chat, the CM called Bhavsar to his room and asked him to show us the material that had been written about him. Bhavsar took us to his cabin. On his table were printouts of stories published by *Tehelka* and the *Hindu* on the CM. I enquired about them to which Bhavsar replied that the CM had too many enemies. I think I almost heard Mike chuckle. Later we were shown the various books the CM had authored and made to listen to recordings of his speeches in India and around the world.

Bhavsar asked me to get a copy of all of them as it would help in my film making. I said I would do so on my next visit. We went back home and Mike packed his bags, he had a flight to catch to Delhi. I hugged him as I called him a cab to the airport. Minutes later Mike called to tell me that he could not locate a single rupee in his pocket when he reached the airport and the taxi driver did not just waive the fare but also gave him Rs 200 for his journey. Mike said this was what he wanted to take away from Gujarat. I agreed wholeheartedly. That was the last time I saw Mike and I am sure wherever he is, he will remember Maithili, his older sister and comrade-in-arms.

I called up Shoma and gave her the details right after. She asked me if I had questioned the CM about the riots. 'Come on Shoma, that's the last thing I would do on my first visit,' I retorted.

Later in the evening I got a call from Shoma saying, 'Come back to Delhi, Rana'. I had just about started to protest when she said she would explain once I was back.

The next morning I reached Delhi and went straight to the *Tehelka* office. I had transferred the footage of the Modi recording to my laptop. Tarun was in his cabin. Shoma joined him. I showed them the footage and they laughed looking at the books by Obama.

'So, why was I called back?'I asked. 'His office will call me in a few days and I am supposed to meet him again.'

Tarun said, 'Look Rana, after the *Tehelka* sting on Bangaru Laxman they shut our office. Modi is all set to be the most powerful man, the PM. If we touch him we will be finished.'

I was not convinced. Was the entire sting operation not a big risk in itself? But I was given a sharp No to every argument.

The same evening Sanjay Bhavsar called me. I let the

phone ring. He called three times and then left a text that the CM would love to see me the following Sunday. I went to a local PCO and called Bhavsar to tell him that I was in Delhi and that a relative had passed away and I was required in the city. I assured him however that I would get back to him in a week's time. Two days later I removed the Uninor sim card from my phone, crushed it and threw it in the dustbin. I did the same with the phone. Maithili made an exit forever that day. The editors took a call that the investigation would not be published.

I have remained silent since.

Till now.

Printed in Great Britain
by Amazon